GREEK
MYTHOLOGY

TEXT
MARILENA CARABATEA
Archaeologist

NOTE TO THE READER

Hermes and Epimetheus. (Detail from a volute krater, c. 440 BC. Oxford 525.)

This book is a brief presentation of Greek mythology aimed at giving the general reading public the opportunity to get to know a basic chapter of Ancient Greek civilisation. It contains accounts of the most important cycles of mythology (the Creation of the World, Herakles, Theseus, the Trojan War) and also examines their possible interpretations. The first four chapters are supplemented by a detailed index containing the names of the most popular gods and heroes in alphabetical order. Readers may turn to this to gain a better understanding of the character of the gods or to supplement their knowledge concerning the events that marked the lives of some of the heroes and the history of their homelands. The tables at the end of the book form another point of reference, clarifying the genealogical trees and relationships between the main ruling families in Greek mythology. It should be stressed that it is not the purpose of this book to give a detailed account of all the different versions of the myths that have been created from ancient times to the present day; it is designed rather to introduce anyone interested to the world of mythology in a very simple, readily comprehensible manner. Its contents are based mainly on the most prevalent versions of the myths, as preserved through the written sources and art, and with frequent references to the plots of ancient Greek tragedy. This brief tour of the world of gods and heroes is completed by an epilogue that takes the form of a brief review drawing attention to reurring motifs in Greek mythology.

Hades, Hermes and Persephone watch the torment of Sisyphus. (Amphora, c. 510 BC. British Museum B 261.)

Herakles relieves Atlas of his burden by taking the vault of heaven on to his shoulders. (Metope from the temple of Zeus at Olympia, c. 470-456 BC.) Left: detail.

I would like to close his note by thanking the archaeologist Maya Komvou, who patiently read the text of the book and made some important comments, and also professors Dimitris Pandermalis and Nikolaos Yalouris for kindly making available some important material. I also wish to thank the staff of Adam Editions, who produced this book.

Athena watches Herakles wrestling with the Lernaian Hydra. (Lekythos, c. 500-490 BC. Paris, Louvre CA 598.)

CONTENTS

INTRODUCTION TO MYTH, ITS TRANSMISSION AND SIGNIFICANCE

MYTHOLOGY is the science or study of myths. A myth may be a story inspired by either real or imaginary events. Today we use the word myth to refer to legendary tales praising the feats of heroes who wrestle with demons and with real or supernatural forces, and who sacrifice themselves for their country and their ideals. The myths of ancient Greece had a similar content, though their significance was very different and much broader.

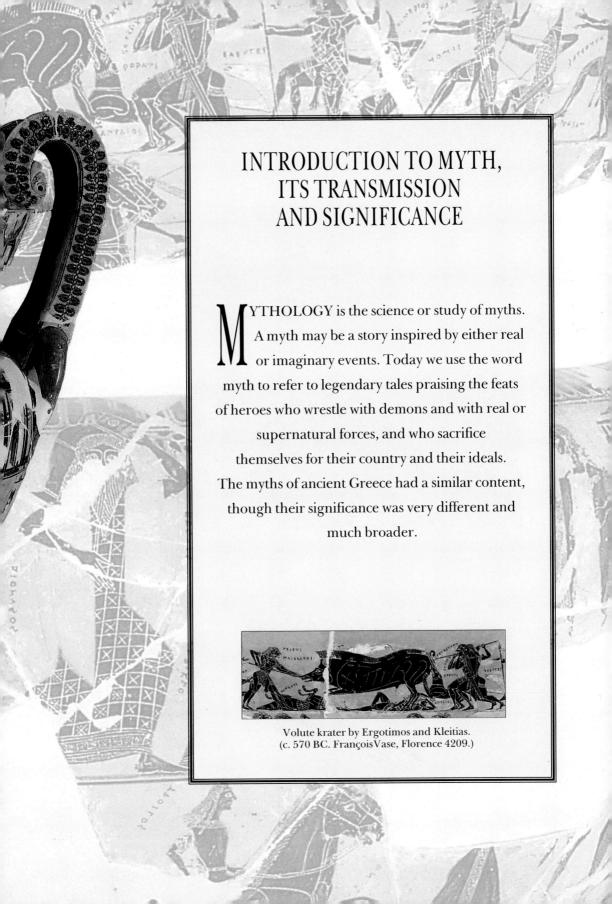

Volute krater by Ergotimos and Kleitias.
(c. 570 BC. François Vase, Florence 4209.)

The hunt for the Kalydonian boar.

Troilos, on horseback, tries to escape Achilles who is chasing him.

Demeter, Dionysos, the three Hours and Zeus arrive at the wedding of Peleus and Thetis.

Hermes and two women watch Achilles attacking Troilos.

Sphinx

THE FRANÇOIS VASE
has impressive
decoration with
mythological
scenes inspired by
the epic tradition.
(c. 570 BC. Florence,
Archaeological
Museum 4209.)

Chariot race in honour of Patroklos.

Thetis, in the house
of Peleus, welcomes
the guests as they
arrive at their
wedding.

1

1 Horseman in the Panathenaic procession in honour of the goddess Athena. (Detail from the south frieze of the Parthenon, c. 447-432 BC. British Museum.)

The older a civilisation, the likelier it is that myths form an inseparable part of its history and religion. Primitive man invented myths to interpret the 'mysteries' of his daily experience, in order to defend himself and adapt to his environment. As he devised ways to meet the basic requirements for his survival (a place to live and food to eat), he began to attempt to interpret those forces that directly affected his life but which he could not control. His inability to find any logical explanation for, and his need to understand, all the factors that sometimes made his daily life easier and sometimes more difficult, led him to attribute them to superior powers, which he embodied in the gods and heroes. Human interest in subjects such as the creation of the world, life after death, and natural phenomena is a feature of most ancient civilisations, and is clear from the vast body of myths that have been preserved to the present day. Similarities can often be discerned between the myths of different peoples, a circumstance which may be attributed either to the fact that people react in similar ways to similar conditions, whether climatological or political, or to cultural exchanges resulting from the development of trade and travel.

It will be useful to begin by examining the sources from which our knowledge of myths is derived. Greek mythology has been preserved to the present day through the writings of ancient authors and through art. Heroic tales were originally sung by bards in the palaces of the Mycenaean kings (14th-11th c. BC). About the 10th century BC, the Ionians of Asia Minor began to compose longer poems about the lives and achievements of their heroes, thus giving birth to epic poetry. This tradition culminated in the *Iliad* and the *Odyssey*, the works of Homer, which date from about the middle of the 8th c. BC.

The *Iliad* records the events that unfolded in the tenth year of the Achaian expedition against Troy. The purpose of this expedition was to restore the honour of Menelaos, the king of Sparta, and return his wife, the famous 'fair Helen', to her homeland, from where she had been abducted by Paris-Alexander, son of Priam, the king of Troy.

The *Odyssey* focuses on one of the heroes of the Trojan War, Odysseus, and narrates his adventures on his return journey to his homeland, Ithake. In his poems, Homer mentions a great number of heroes and gives us their family trees, but he does not show the same interest in the origins and genealogies of the gods. On the contrary, he accepts the order in the divine world as given, and frequently refers to divine intervention affecting the actions of men; this is clear in the *Iliad*, where the gods are divided into two groups: those who protect the Achaians and those who support the Trojans (see p. 159).

The question of the creation of the gods and the world attracted the interest of another poet, Hesiod of Boeotia, who was probably a contemporary of Homer. In his poem *Theogony*, Hesiod sets out the genealogy of the gods and narrates the events that led to the establishing of the power of the twelve Olympian gods; in another poem, entitled *Works and Days*, he describes the creation of the human race.

Originally the poems of Homer and Hesiod were recited by rhapsodes at fairs and in the courts of kings. This oral tradition naturally gave rise to many

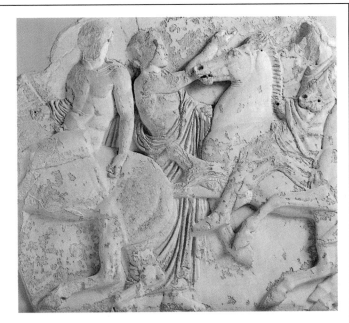

different versions, though the basic plot of the story did not change. The transmission of the Homeric poems acquired great importance in Athens in the 6th c. BC. Solon was probably the first to have them written down and made the teaching of them part of the education of young Athenians. After him, Peisistratos also introduced the recitation of the Homeric poems into the Panathenaia, the major festival in honour of Athena, the patron goddess of the city, which was celebrated every four years. This led to a wider audience for the rhapsodes, and intensified the influence of the Homeric poems both on other epic poets and on lyric and tragic poetry, which evolved in the 6th and 5th c. BC respectively.

Attic art of the Archaic (6th c. BC) and particularly of the Clas-

2. Horseman in the Panathenaic procession. (Detail from the north frieze of the Parthenon, c. 447-432 BC. British Museum.)

sical (5th c. BC) periods confirms the popularity of the epic tradition. The founders of ancient tragedy, Aeschylus, Sophocles and Euripides, often drew their inspiration from episodes taken from the epic narrative, which they embellished or modified in varying degrees, depending on the requirements of the play. At the same time, the figures of the gods and heroes were predominant in the repertoire of Attic art from as early as the first decades of the 6th c. BC. Vase-painters, sculptors and painters for the most part selected myths that were familiar to their contemporaries. To read the picture adorning a vase, or a piece of sculpture, it is necessary first

1. Zeus about to throw the thunderbolt. (Bronze statuette, 5th c. BC. Athens, National Archaeological Museum 16546.)

of all to know the basic elements of the story, and then to decipher the established conventions that identify the individual figures. The most popular figures in myth are normally accompanied by their personal symbols: Zeus, for example, holds the thunderbolt, or Herakles wears the lion's pelt and a quiver full of arrows, and carries a

club (see pp. 53-55). In some cases, too, the scenes are accompanied by inscriptions giving the names of the characters depicted. In the absence of these elements, the modern viewer, at least, is obliged to guess at the identity of some of the figures on the basis of the contextual evidence. Here, ancient observers were at an advantage and probably better able to understand the meaning of a scene, since they had more points of reference.

From the period during which epic poetry evolved, which is known as the Heroic period, myths played an important role in ancient education, and also in the development of ancient Greek society, since they cultivated the belief that the events hymned by Homer and the other epic poets were an account of the glorious past of Greece. Many prose works entitled *Genealogies and Histories*, which date from the late 6th and 5th c. BC, are attributed to the so-called historiographers. These writers were influenced by the epic tradition and wrote genealogies in their attempt to seek the roots of contemporary history in the heroic past, and thereby demonstrate the continuity of Greek civilisation. Some of them, indeed, rationalised the traditional myths in order to confirm their authenticity. Hekataios of Miletos, for example, (c. 500 BC) states that Kerberos was not the terrifying dog of tradition,

2

which had three heads and vigilantly guarded the gates of Hades, but a snake which was called 'the dog of Hades', since its bite led to death.

Despite this, the first doubts as to the historical value of myth were expressed in antiquity. The first to raise serious objections to the credibility of Hesiod's narrative of the creation of the world were the pre-Socratic philosophers (c. 6th c. BC), who sought to identify the beginnings of things in the natural elements, such as water, air and fire. It was not only philosophical thought, however, that dealt a blow to the authenticity of the myths. In the 5th c. BC, Herodotus, who is known as the 'father of history', makes his position clear, and says that the stories he tells are not myths, but real events which he either experienced himself or heard from eye witnesses. Mod-

ern scholarship, however, has demonstrated that some of Herodotus's accounts could better be described as 'legends and traditions' than as historical events.

The first to write history in the modern sense of the word was Thucydides, who describes the events of the Peloponnesian War (431-404 BC) in his *Histories*. Even Thucydides, however, who was dealing with actual events and was aware of the nature of the historian's task, does not dispute the historicity of the events narrated in the Homeric poems. Moreover, the case of Troy, still occupies modern students. The theory that the epic poems are an expression of the ideals of a heroic age and do not relate to real events, was shaken by the excavations of Heinrich Schliemann, who brought to light the ruins of Troy and Mycenae. The existing evidence, of course, does not confirm that the Achaians really did launch an expedition against Troy, much less that the cause of the war was the abduction of the 'fair Helen'. The substantiation of some of the elements of myth by the excavation evidence, however, is an indication that the boundaries between myth and history cannot always be drawn with complete certainty.

From the 5th century BC onwards, belief in myths was increasingly shaken. At the end of the century, Plato asserted that in an ideal state myths should be

2 Female figure holding a torch and an oinochoe. The torch is regarded as the symbol of Demeter and Persephone, but in the absence of an inscription the figure cannot certainly be identified. (Fragment of a pelike, c. 450-425 BC. Elis, Archaeological Collection.)

1. Heinrich Schliemann. (1822-1890).

used only as an educational tool to form a person's character, and he accordingly rejects all those myths that in his opinion did not constitute suitable moral precepts. In the 4th c. BC, Aristotle described mythology as a different way of thinking, and stressed that the predominant element in philosophy was reason. Greek mythology nevertheless attracted the interest of many writers in the Hellenistic and Roman periods. We may cite by way of example Diodorus Siculus (c. 50-30), who regarded the heroes as historical figures, and also the work of two travellers, the *Geography* of Strabo (c. AD 20-27) and the *Description of Greece* by Pausanias (2nd c. AD), who wrote down the myths they were told in the various places they visited. Finally, Apollodoros compiled his *Library*, in the 1st c. AD. Since this book contains most of the Greek myths, it has proved of great value for the study of the ancient world.

To sum up, it should be stressed that what is today called mythology and deemed a collection of imaginary stories, was one of the corner-stones of ancient Greek civilisation. First, it formed the basis of ancient Greek religion: it was through myths that the gods were established as superior powers who ruled the entire world, imposed order and justice, and determined the fate of every human being. The myths also sang the praises of a glorious past, since they extolled the feats of the heroes and therefore promoted the high ideals of courage, self-sacrifice and patriotism. From the time of Homer until at least the Classical period, the heroes were respected as models, and the prevailing view was that every generation ought to make some significant contribution to the completion of the historical structure, so as to serve as an example for its descendants and honour the civilisation it had inherited. These views and beliefs survived for many centuries. Even in the progressive Athens of the Classical period, in which there were intellectuals like Euripides, who disputed the historicity of the Trojan War, and Thucydides, who wrote 'real history', there was a firmly rooted belief that the Athenians were autochthonous, that is that they were descended from King Ke-

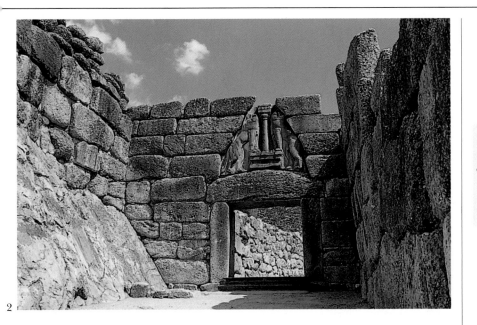

2. The Lion Gate on the acropolis at Mycenae. (13th-11th c.BC.)

krops who was born from the soil of Attica.

It might be supposed that in the ancient world myth functioned as a means of interpreting reality. The ancient Greeks used important events as sources of inspiration for the creation of myths; a story based either on reality or on imaginary events, or (as was probably usually the case) on both, was passed from mouth to mouth, gaining credibility and finally establishing itself as important knowledge. It is symptomatic that the majority, if not all, of the Greek cities had a foundation myth; the foundation of most of the cities is an established historical fact, but the authenticity of the myth linked with it cannot be substantiated.

One interesting theory draws a parallel between the first steps of civilisation and the first steps of human beings. Most children in the world grow up with fairy tales and often make up their own imaginary stories; this is probably a method of adapting to reality. The evolution of civilisation follows a similar course: at first people idealise nature, their past, and their experiences, in order to defend themselves against anything unknown, of which they are afraid. Gradually, however, they acquire greater knowledge and use their reason to account for both natural phenomena and also their personal experiences. As their thinking matures, they distinguish myth from reality, acquire a sense of history, and free themselves of the ghosts of the 'heroic age'.

THE CREATION OF THE WORLD

THE OLDEST complete work on the creation of the world and the establishment of order amongst the society of the gods is the *Theogony*, by the Boeotian poet Hesiod, which dates from about 700 BC. Creation myths, however, have been preserved in many versions both earlier and later than Hesiod, and reference will briefly be made to the most important features of them.

Poseidon, Apollo and Artemis. (Part of the east frieze of the Parthenon, c. 447-432 BC. Athens, Acropolis Museum.)

THE GODS

According to Hesiod, the beginning of creation starts with Chaos, Gaia (Earth) and Eros. Erebos and Night were born from Chaos, while Ouranos and Okeanos sprang from Gaia. The role of Ouranos was at first to cover and therefore to protect Gaia, but he then coupled with her and they became the first gods to rule the world. From their union were born the twelve Titans (Okeanos, Koios, Kreios, Hyperion, Iapetos, Kronos, Theia, Rhea, Themis, Mnemosyne, Phoibe and Tethys), the three Kyklopes (Brontes, Steropes and Arges), and, finally, the three hundred-handed giants

1. Rhea deceives Kronos with a stone wrapped in baby clothes. (Column krater, c. 460 BC. Louvre G 366.)

(Kottos, Gyges and Briares). Ouranos did not welcome his offspring, however, because he did not want to lose his throne when they grew up, and to prevent this he made his wife hide their children deep in her bowels. Motherly instinct overcame conjugal solidarity, however, and Gaia decided to deploy her female wiles and intelligence in order to free her children. The only way to achieve this aim was to take away her husband's strength and she therefore armed her youngest child, Kronos, with a sickle and arranged a suitable moment for him to cut of his father's genitals. From the seed of Ouranos, which fell into the sea, was born Aphrodite, while from his blood, which was spilt on the earth, were created the Fates, the Giants, and the Meliai Nymphs.

Kronos succeeded his father and took his sister Rhea as his wife; he then freed the rest of his brothers from the bowels of the earth and shared some of his power with them: to Okeanos, who married Tethys, was assigned the task of ruling over the sea and rivers, while Hyperion and Phoibe assumed responsibility for guiding the sun and the stars. The inevitable happened, however, and Kronos was consumed by the same fears that had tormented Ouranos. When Rhea presented him with their first child, he felt his throne threatened, and decided

2

to swallow all his children (Hestia, Demeter, Hera, Hades, Poseidon and Zeus) so that they could never dethrone him. Once again it was the mother who opposed the ambitions of the powerful father. Rhea managed to save her youngest child, Zeus, deceiving her husband with a stone wrapped in swaddling clothes. Kronos swallowed the stone unsuspectingly, and Zeus was brought up on Mount Dikte in Crete in the care of the

2-3. Aphrodite, Poseidon, Demeter, Athena, Zeus, Hera, Apollo and Artemis. (Circular marble altar or base, c. 350-340 BC. Athens, National Archaeological Museum 1731.)

3

Nymphs, while the Kouretes danced and clashed their shields to cover the sound of his crying, and Amaltheia, who is described variously as a goat or a Nymph, suckled him with her milk. In time Zeus grew to manhood and became strong enough to dethrone his father and compel him to spew the rest of his children from his entrails.

It was now the turn of Zeus to rule the world. He married his sister, Hera, and divided his realm into three kingdoms: he himself remained lord of the sky and established himself on Mount Olympos, assigning to Poseidon the task of ruling the sea and to Hades the kingdom of the Underworld. He also honoured his two sisters with divine duties, appointing Demeter goddess of agriculture and Hestia goddess of the family hearth. After this, Zeus gradually formed the group of twelve gods who would dwell with him on Mount Olympos. This group initially included Hera, the goddess of marriage and wife of Zeus, Poseidon and Demeter. To these were later added his most important children: Athena, the goddess of wisdom, who sprang from his head; Apollo, the god of music, and Artemis, the goddess of hunting, who were born of the union between Zeus and Leto; Aphrodite, the goddess of love, who emerged from the seed of Ouranos that fell into the sea; his two sons by Hera: Hephaistos, the god of metallurgy, and Ares, the god of war; Hermes, the messenger of the gods, whom he bore by the Nymph Maia; and finally, Dionysos, the god of wine and merry-making, who was the fruit of his love for Semele. The twelve Olympian gods are assembled in the depiction on the east pediment of the Parthenon, where they watch the ceremonial of the Panathenaia, the festival in honour of Athena. In this scene, as in others, they are represented

1

as idealised human figures, and identified by their personal symbols.

THE BATTLE OF THE TITANS

Zeus's ascent to the throne was not universally accepted: Gaia encouraged the Titans, the brothers of Kronos, to revolt and overthrow the new regime.

Zeus and the other members of the Olympic pantheon fortified themselves on Mount Olympos to defend their kingdom. They finally managed to defeat the Titans, but only after winning over the other children of Ouranos and Gaia, the Kyklopes and the hundred-handed giants. Despite the defeat of the Titans, Gaia refused to be reconciled, and next aroused the Giants against the gods of Mount Olympos.

THE BATTLE OF THE GIANTS

The Giants are described either as terrible monsters with serpents on their head, a human body and a serpent-tail instead of legs, or as fully armed warriors; in both cases, however, they are regarded as savage beings who do not obey the laws and rules. They attacked the gods on Mount Olympos, throwing stones, trees and fire-brands at them, and at the same time upset the order of the world by moving mountains, plunging islands to the depths of the sea, and changing the course of rivers. The gods joined forces in order to confront them; they were finally victorious only when Herakles entered the struggle and Zeus managed to prevent Gaia from getting the magic herb that made the giants invincible.

1-2. Athena and a Giant who has fallen to the ground. Scene from the Battle of the Giants from the pediment of a temple on the Acropolis. (c. 535-520 BC. Acropolis Museum.)

2

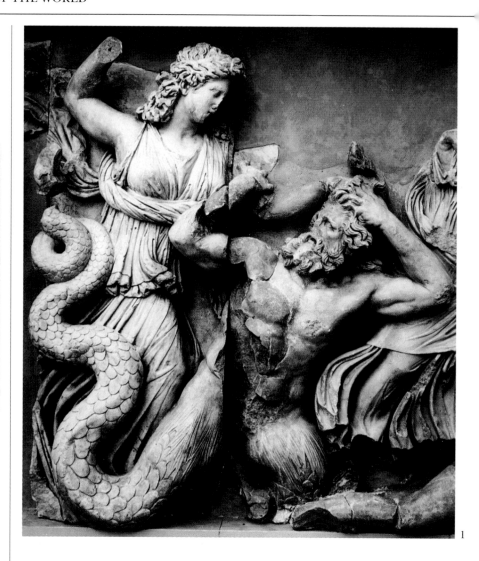

1-2. The Battle of the Giants. The Giants are depicted with serpents' legs and human form. (Detail from the frieze of the Pergamon Altar, which was dedicated to Zeus. c. 180-150 BC. Berlin, Staatliche Museen.)

1

All these events, which were played out before the Olympic pantheon was finally established, mark periods of great upheaval in the world. The Giants were said to be so powerful that they could moved mountains and change the course of rivers; indeed, according to one version of the Battle of the Giants, Poseidon lifted up an entire island (Nisyros) in order to throw it at his opponents. Since all these episodes are reminiscent of disasters that we now know can be caused by phenomena such as earthquakes, floods, etc., we may assume that stories of this kind give expression to man's need to interpret what is

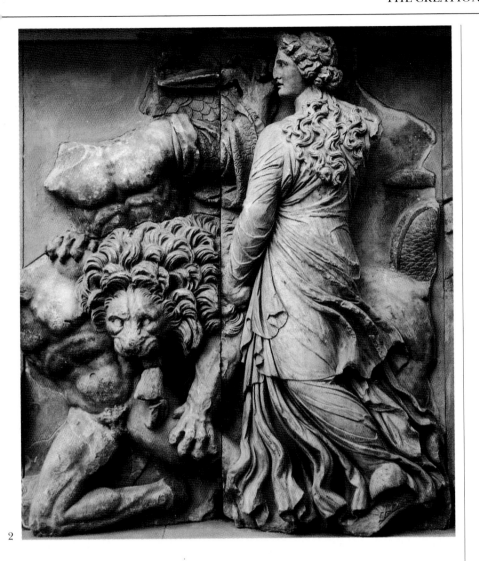

2

happening in nature. At the same time, however, it has been asserted that the myths dealing with the long conflicts between the gods also have a symbolical significance. The antagonism of Ouranos and Kronos towards their children perhaps alludes to the struggle between the generations, and the inability of the older generation to give place to the younger. The Battle of the Titans and the Battle of the Giants possibly hint at the conflict between two opposed worlds, with the Titans and Giants on the one hand, representing lawless, anarchical societies, and chaos, while the Olympian gods, on the other, are presented as the defenders of natural order and balance. The victory of the gods therefore involves not only the establishment of their power and their worship, but also the triumph of civilisation and order over savagery and anarchy.

The twelve gods who established themselves on Mount Olympos ruled the world more democratically than their forefathers. Zeus made himself supreme ruler of the gods and men, but also shared his power with his brothers and sisters, and assigned certain duties to minor deities. Whoever occupied a place amongst the gods was completely responsible for his own actions and decisions. Poseidon could cause a storm or calm the sea for sailors to voyage on, Demeter ensured the fertility of the earth, Apollo gave oracles and taught music, Aphrodite spread love, Dionysos gave men courage for war, Athena enlightened the world through her wisdom, Hera protected married life and Hephaistos taught the crafts. At the same time, however, Zeus reserved the right to impose order and

1-4. Battle of the Giants. (Amphora, c. 400-390 BC. Louvre s 1667.).

1. Zeus threatens the enemy with his thunderbolt, while Nike drives his chariot and Dionysos fights from a chariot drawn by panthers

2. Poseidon, mounted on horseback and carrying his trident, Athena with her spear, and Herakles with his sword, put their foes to rout.

often intervened with his thunderbolt to resolve major disputes between the immortals; for, as we shall see below, the ancient Greeks gave their gods not only human form, but also human weaknesses. Many myths accordingly refer to the peccadillos and errors of the gods, which, of course, are punished according to the laws of justice and ethics.

This is the picture of the Greek pantheon to be formed from the evidence derived from ancient art and literature. The view that natural phenomena, the main-tenance of balance in the world, and human destiny depend on the power and will of the gods demonstrates the human need to comprehend the forces that pull the strings of life. The same reasoning might be used to interpret the weaknesses attributed to the otherwise omnipotent deities. The belief that the immortals who rule the world can feel envy, pain, grief, or love helped people to come to terms with their emotions, which they could not always interpret rationally. Many myths were thus woven around the jealousy and

3

4

3. Apollo shoots his accurate arrows, and Artemis menacingly raises two lighted torches.

4. Ares, in a chariot driven by Aphrodite, and the two Dioskouroi, on horseback, threaten the Giants with their spears, while Persephone fights with sword in hand.

1-3. Part of the north frieze of the Treasury of the Siphnians at Delphi, c. 530 BC.

Ares and Hermes fight two Giants each.

Apollo and Artemis fight with three Giants.

The lions drawing the chariot of Kybele are savaged by a Giant.

vengeful nature of Hera and the infidelities of Zeus, Demeter mourns the loss of her daughter, Persephone, like any mother, and Poseidon does everything he can to win the heart of Amphitrite and make her his wife.

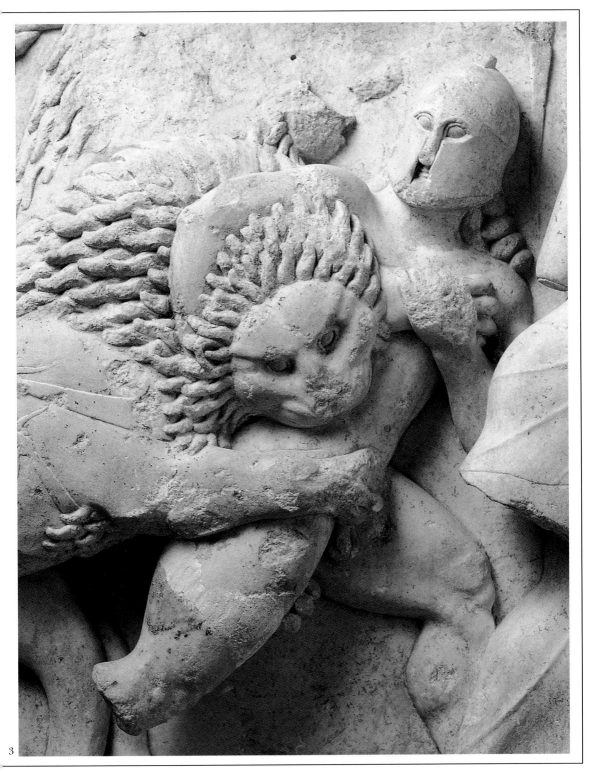

3

MANKIND

1-2. Herakles kills Zeus's eagle with his arrow in order to free Prometheus. (Krater, c. 610 BC. Athens, National Archaeological Museum 16384.)

The gods created human beings and other living creatures from a basic compound of earth and fire, to which they added whatever other materials could be mixed with it. They then gave Prometheus and Epimetheus, the sons of the Titan Iapetos and the Okeanid Klymene, the task of endowing their creations with gifts (Plato, *Protagoras* 320c-322a). The two brothers agreed that Epimetheus should apportion the gifts, and should later call upon Prometheus to oversee his work. Epimetheus called upon all his wisdom to endow all creatures with the appropriate means to ensure their survival and perpetuation; he gave some of them fur, for example, and others wings to fly, and made some of them eaters of grass and others eaters of plants. When it came to man's turn, however, Epimetheus had run out of gifts, and man therefore remained naked and defenceless against nature.

Prometheus felt responsible for his brother's mistake and tried to find some way to help mankind. Since the gifts offered by the gods had been used up, he had to think of something else. Prometheus decided secretly to enter the workshop of Hephaistos and Athena and steal fire. It was a very bold plan, but proved effective: Prometheus not only gave fire to humans, but also taught them how to use it. From this sprang the art of metal-working which made an important contribution to the development of civilisation. Zeus, however, did not want to give mortals the power of fire, and when he saw what had happened, his anger was uncontrollable. He determined to punish Prometheus severely, and ordered him to be taken to the East, and chained to a crag in the Caucasus, where every morning he sent an eagle to devour his liver, which grew whole again during the night (Apollodoros, *Library* 1.7.1). Many years later Herakles freed him from his torment by killing the eagle with his arrows (Aeschylus, *Prometheus Bound* 436-506).

The stories of Epimetheus and Prometheus complete the cycle of creation myths: the error made by the former and the daring of the latter are an attempt to account for the differences between humans and other living beings. Furthermore, Prometheus was punished in order restore justice because, whatever his motives, he had violated Zeus's commands and the laws against crimes such as theft and impiety. When Herakles finally put an end to his torment, we may assume that this, too, is at the decision of Zeus who, of course, had not taken pity on Prometheus but probably wanted to give the pan-Hellenic hero yet another opportunity to demonstrate his prowess.

As with most traditions relating to the history of the creation of mankind, the first woman was created after the man in Greek mythology, too, and in this case she was called Pandora, meaning the one who brings gifts. The birth of Pandora was a popular subject in Attic iconography. On a volute krater in Oxford (see pp. 34-35) Pandora is depicted from the waist up as she springs from the earth and is welcomed by Epimetheus, while Eros, flying between them, hints at their future relationship, and the scene is watched by Hermes and Zeus. The hammer held by Epimetheus indicates that he is a craftsman, and this specific scene may therefore be inspired by the version of myth according to which woman was created by Epimetheus.

Hesiod (*Works and Days* 42-105) recounts another version of the myth, in which Zeus created woman in order to punish men for accepting the gift of fire from Prometheus, and gave the other gods the task of adorning her to make her beautiful and alluring. He called his creation Pandora and sent her to Epimetheus, together with a

1

2

jar that was to remain forever sealed. Epimetheus, of course, could not resist a gift of this nature, even though his brother had warned him never to accept any presents from Zeus. The pair lived happily until Pandora was overcome by curiosity and decided to open the jar; then all the misfortunes of the world sprang from it: illnesses, war, misery and death. The woman was terrified at the spectacle before her and immediately closed the jar, but it was too late, for all that remained inside was Hope, which was at the bottom.

Hesiod interpreted the unpleasant things that happened in the world as the result of Zeus's vengeance. He represents the omnipotent god as being in competition with weak mortals: Zeus was obliged to cede to mankind the fire that had been stolen by Prometheus, but took his revenge by sending woman to them, who was to be the source of all misfortunes. His choice of this version of the myth reveals Hesiod to be a misogynist and a pessimist, since it depicts mankind as being entrapped by the god's anger. A similar pessimism characterises Hesiod's account of the first five races of man (*Works and Days* 109-201), which succeeded each other until they had completed their cycle, when they were covered by the earth. The first to come into the world was the golden race, which was blessed and lived in a perfect society in which there were no problems. There followed a silver race, which was not worthy of its predecessor, since it committed terrible crimes and neglected the sacrifices to the gods. Next came the brazen race, which was interested only in war and ultimately destroyed itself. It was succeeded by the race of heroes, who were created from the earth and were the predecessors of mankind; they too, however were destroyed in heroic conflicts such as the Trojan War. Last came the iron race, which lived with its problems and illnesses and was destroyed by corruption and lack of respect for the family, justice and, of course, the gods. Quite apart from the possibility that Hesiod's sequence of races hints at actual catastrophes, it should be noted that the last two races correspond to historically documented periods, known as the Bronze Age and the Iron Age, since they are characterised by the use of these two metals.

The idea of the complete destruction of the world is found not only in the writing of Hesiod, but also in myths relating to the terrible floods that wiped out the human race. The most famous of these is the so-called flood of Deukalion (Apollodoros, *Library* 1.7.2-4), the only survivors of which were Deukalion, the son of Prometheus, and his wife Pyrrha, who was the daughter of Epimetheus and Pandora. They survived because they heeded their parents' warnings and built an ark to save themselves. The story to this point is parallel with the story of the flood of Noah in the Old Testament, but naturally the two have different endings. When the flood came to an end, Deukalion's ark was on the summit of Mount Parnassos, where the two survivors made sacrifices to give thanks to Zeus for their delivery and to pray for the renewal of the human race. The gods heard their prayers and told them to throw stones over their shoulders; from the stones thrown by Deukalion sprang men, and from those thrown by Pyrrha women.

We may end this chapter on the creation of mankind with a brief reference to the origins of the Greeks. According to one version of the myth, the founding-father of the Greeks was Hellen, the son of Deukalion and Pyrrha. Hellen had three sons: Doros, who became the founding-father of the Dorians, Aiolos,

The Titans Atlas and Prometheus suffer the eternal punishments imposed upon them by Zeus. The former supports the vault of heaven on his shoulders and the latter is chained to a crag in the Caucasus, while every day an eagle devours his liver. (Lakonian kylix, c. 570-560 BC. Vatican, Gregoriano Etrusco Museum 16592.)

from whom were descended the Aiolians, and Xouthos; the last married Kreousa, daughter of Erechtheus, King of Athens, by whom he had two sons, Ion and Achaios, who became the founder of the Ionians and the Achaians respectively. Hellen's sisters coupled with Zeus: Pandora (the grand-daughter of the first woman) bore Graikos, and Thyia bore Magnes, the forefather of the Magnesians and the Macedonians. This myth gives expression to the belief that the founders of the most important tribes that dwelt in Greece were descendants of Deukalion and Pyrrha, who were in turn descended from primeval divine forces, since their fathers, Prometheus and Epimetheus, were the children of Titans. This belief reflects the tendency of the ancient Greeks to associate their roots with deities who are supposed to rule the world, in order to justify their superiority and supremacy. The coupling of a god with a mortal woman is, moreover, a motif found very commonly in Greek mythology, since divine origins reinforce the prestige and authority of the heroes.

1. The birth of Pandora. (Volute krater, c. 440 BC. Oxford 525.)

2. The Satyrs form Pandora, the first woman sent by Zeus into the world. (Drawing from a vase, 6th c. BC.)

THE LIFE-CYCLE
OF MAN

The twelve Olympian gods ruled the
world, along with many other
deities who determined the fate of
men. Amongst them were the forces that
pulled the strings of the daily lives of
mortals, from the
rising of the sun until its setting,
from birth until death.

Helios rises in his chariot in the East, while the stars sink in
the Ocean. (Kalyx krater, c. 420 BC.
British Museum E 466.)

THE CALENDAR CYCLE

1. The horses from the chariot of Helios. (East pediment of the Parthenon, c. 447-432 BC. British Museum.)

2. Head of Helios. The holes can be seen by which the metal rays were attached. (From a marble statue of the god, 220-180 BC. Rhodes, Archaeological Museum.)

Many versions been preserved of myths relating to solar and astral phenomena, attesting to the fact that man must have been impressed at a very early date by phenomena such as the succession of days and time in general. In the *Theogony* , Hesiod states that Helios (the sun), Selene (the moon) and Eos (the dawn), were the children of two Titans, Hyperion and Theia. Another version of the myth identifies Helios with Apollo and Selene with Artemis, and interprets the arrows of these gods as symbols of the light they radiate.

In art Helios is depicted as a youth, wears his rays as a crown on his head and drives a chariot pulled by winged horses. Every day he travels from one end of the Ocean to the other, starting from the land of the Aithiopes in the East and ending in the land of the Hesperides in the West; on a krater in the British Museum (see pp. 36-37) the stars are depicted as young children diving in the Ocean as Helios pursues his course through the heavens.

When Helios completes his journey Selene bathes in the waters of Ocean, bedecks herself and then ascends into the heavens. She is described as a beautiful young girl who is either mounted on horseback or drives a chariot pulled by winged horses; she is accompanied by a youth, who is none other than Augerinos (the morning and evening star), who brings the stars and heralds the night.

1

The following day-break is brought by Eos, the personification of dawn, accompanied by her son, Eosphoros or Phosphoros. Eosphoros or Phosphoros is identified with the Aposperitis (the evening star) and scholarship has demonstrated that he is also identified with Augerinos, (the morning star) for he is the planet Venus, which is visible only at dawn or in the evening.

When nature has been awakened by the arrival of Eos, Helios again sets out on his journey, having returned during the night from the finishing point to the starting point of his course, that is from the West to the East. Ancient poets describe Helios, wearied at the end of the day, lying and relaxing on a golden bed which, during the course of the Moon's reign in heaven, floats on the waters of Ocean and carries him back to the East.

In the Classical period, Greeks believed that Helios and Selene

2

were only worshipped as gods in barbarian religions, and did not therefore honour them as gods, though they paid them equal respect and were in awe of their power. It is significant that in Modern Greek the expression, 'the sun is ruling' means 'the sun is setting', not that he is a king, and 'I have ruled' is used metaphorically to mean 'I have gone to sleep'. Another ancient view that has survived to the present day relates to the influence of the phases of the moon on the life of humans. In ancient Greece certain political decisions were taken according to the current phase of

1. Torso of Selene. (East pediment of the Parthenon, 447-432 BC. Athens, Acropolis Museum.)

1

2. Selene rises on horseback in the heaven. (Kalyx krater, c. 420 BC. British Museum E 466.)

the moon. Herodotus (6. 106) tells us that the Spartans never set out to war unless the moon was full. And according to Thucydides (7.50. 3-4), when the Athenians, exhausted by battle and illness, were preparing to withdraw their ships from Syracuse during the Peloponnesian War, there was an eclipse of the moon; the prophets interpreted this as a sign from the gods and advised the Athenians not to move for the following twenty-seven days.

The solar cycle is completed by the days, weeks and seasons, which were also personified in mythology. In the *Odyssey* (XII 129) we learn that Helios had sev-en sacred herds, each with 350 cattle, tended by two of his daughters in Thrinakia (modern Sicily); no-one was allowed to slaughter these animals, whose number remained always the same and, perhaps not by chance, coincides with the number of days in a solar year. Similarly, the fifty daughters borne by Selene to her great love, Endymion, should probably be identified with the fifty weeks of the year. Finally, in the traditions created after Hesiod's time, the Hours are represented as four or twelve daughters of Helios, and it may therefore be assumed that they were associated with the seasons of the year and the hours of the day.

THE LIFE OF MAN

Convictions relating to the forces that directly influenced the personal life of every individual were dominated by a belief in the power of destiny. In the *Theogony*, the Fates and the Hours are said to be children of Zeus and Themis. On the François vase they are depicted together with the first gods, attending the wedding of Peleus and the Nereid Thetis, praying and offering gifts to the newly-married couple. There were three Fates: Klotho who spins the thread of life, Lachesis who distributes joy and grief and in general determines the course to be taken by the life of every mortal, and Atropos, who cuts the thread of life and brings death. The Hours, of whom there were also three Eirene, Dike and Eunomia have the task of rewarding men for their industry and virtue and are represented in later writings as the protectors of vegetation and fertility. The gods oversee all actions of mortals, however, and just as they praise good behaviour, so they also punish injustice. This is the task of the Furies, who were born from the blood of Ouranos that fell on to the earth when he was castrated by Kronos. They are depicted as winged female figures with serpents on their heads and arms,

1

2

who pursue and torment murderers (pp. 132-134).

In addition to these three groups of female deities who determine the course of life, and reward and punish, Hesiod mentions many other descendants of the gods who have similar duties; Chaos, who along with Gaia and Eros existed from the beginning of the world, gave birth to Erebos and Night; amongst the children of Night were Nemesis, Hypnos, and Thanatos (see p. 46), Geras (see p. 103), Apate and Iris. The children of Iris were Ponos, Lethe, Limos, Maches, Phonos, Dysnomia and Horkos. And Styx, the daughter of Okeanos gave to the world Kratos, Bia, Zelos and Nike. The personification of abstract concepts representing social values (eg. Kratos), personal experiences (eg. Maches) or feelings (Ponos) in the form of deities related to the ancient gods of the Greek pantheon reflects a tendency on the part of mankind to mythicise those experiences that impress or inspire awe. Consequently the act of deifying these concepts consolidates social values, such as Kratos and Horkos, propitiates misfortunes, such as Limos and Mache, and interprets feelings such as Pothos and Iris.

When the life of man on earth is over, he is taken to his permanent residence in the gloomy kingdom of Hades, which we shall now explore.

THE KINGDOM OF THE UNDERWORLD

1. Hades and Persephone seated on a banquet couch. (Kylix, c. 440-430 BC. British Museum E 82.)

When Zeus established his authority on Mount Olympos, he assigned rule over the Underworld to Pluto-Hades. The poets describe his kingdom as plunged in the darkness of the bowels of the earth; its gates were vigilantly guarded by Kerberos, a terrible dog with three heads and serpents all over his body, who prevented any soul from ever returning to the world of the living.

The powerful Hades dwelt in the Underworld with his wife, Persephone, the beautiful daughter of Zeus and Demeter (for the abduction of Persephone see pp. 170-173). He is normally represented as a venerable bearded man holding a royal sceptre or a libation vase. He is also identified with Pluto, the god of wealth, whose symbol is a cornucopia. Pluto is said to have been the son of Demeter and Iasion, and to have been brought up by Eirene; originally he bestowed his gifts only on virtuous mortals, but was blinded by Zeus and obliged to distribute wealth at random. The association of death and wealth in the person of a single god is

1

2. Demeter, goddess of agriculture, holds the plough, and Pluto, the god of prosperity, the cornucopia. (Pelike, c. 440-430 BC. Athens, National Archaeological Museum 16346.)

probably an expression of man's attempt to come to terms with death; the identification of the god who rules men's souls with the god of prosperity relieves the misfortune brought by the former through the happiness distributed by the latter. The painter Polygnotos depicted the kingdom of Hades in the first half of the 5th c. BC in a wall-painting that adorned the Club of the Knidians at Delphi. Although this painting has not survived, we know its content from the detailed description given by the traveller Pausanias in the 2nd c. AD (*Description of Greece* 10.28.2); and the same subject was quite popular in Attic sculpture and vase-painting in the Classical period (5th c. BC). All this evidence allows us to reconstruct the beliefs of the ancient Greeks relating to the journey of souls.

When Atropos decided to cut the thread of a man's life, his soul had to be taken to the kingdom of Hades. Some ancient depictions, inspired by epic narratives, portray Hypnos and Thanatos as winged youths removing the body of a dead warrior from the field of battle. The souls of the dead became the charge of Hermes Psychopompos, who either took them to the gates of Hades or delivered them to Charon. Every soul had to have an obol in its mouth to pay the fare for Charon's boat,

1. Hypnos and Thanatos carry the body of a dead warrior from the battlefield. (Kylix, c. 500-490 BC. British Museum E 12.)

which transported it to the gates of the Underworld by way of the river Acheron and Lake Acherousia. When the souls arrived at their destination they underwent a trial, which evaluated their actions and decided their fate in the life eternal. The official judges of Hades were Minos, Rhadamanthys and Aiakos, whose lives were distinguished by outstanding honour and wisdom. Those souls who were adjudged honourable drank of the waters of the river Lethe, so as to forget their unpleasant experiences, and were taken to the Elysian Fields, where they found peace and tranquillity. The souls who were found to have been unjust and dishon-

ourable, on the other hand, were handed over to the Furies (Alekto, Tisiphone and Megaira) and taken to Tartaros to suffer condign punishment. Finally, those who had dared to insult the gods were condemned to eternal torment.

A good example of the last is Sisyphos, who was said to have managed to cheat Death twice. On the first occasion he chained Death up, so that no-one died on earth until Ares managed to free him and restore order. On the second occasion, Sisyphos passed through the gates of Hades, but had given his wife instructions to abstain from the customary offerings to the gods of the Underworld; he then used this as a means of persuading Persephone to permit him to go back up to earth, so that the traditional sacrifices would be resumed. He remained there for several more years, since Death did not dare to approach him again. Sisyphos finally died very old and weary, but was severely punished for his double act of impiety: he was condemned to push a large rock up a hill, which rolled back down as soon as he reached the top. On an amphora in the British Museum Sisyphos's torment is watched by Hades, Hermes and Persephone. Another example is Salmoneus who dared to claim that he was Zeus, and therefore was perpetually threatened by a rock hanging over his head; Tityos had once slighted either Hera or Leto and was therefore chained forever while a vulture ate his liver; Ixion was bound to a wheel that turned ceaselessly, because he had attempted to seduce Hera; and Tantalos was tortured by eternal thirst and hunger, because he had dared to test the gods by offering them his own son for dinner.

It may be concluded from these myths that the souls of the honourable were regarded as examples for imitation, while those of the less honourable act-ed as deterrents. The concept of eternal punishment, however, is probably a reflection of the vanity of life on earth, which consists of a continuous struggle against death and the difficulties ordained by destiny.

2. Hades, Hermes and Persephone watch the torment of Sisyphos. (Amphora, c. 510 BC. British Museum B 261.)

2

HEROES

T HE FEATS of the heroes are sung in epic poetry, which was composed by Homer and other, now unknown, poets. The heroes were distinguished from ordinary mortals by their exceptional courage and moral character. They were inferior to the gods, however, because they were not immortal.

Herakles kills the Lernaian Hydra.
(Frieze slab, 1st c. AD. Delphi Museum.)

INTRODUCTION

Heroes were mortals who played leading roles in Greek mythology. Their personality was compounded of a variety of elements. First of all, a mortal's heroism and strength may be due to his divine origins, since heroes were often the offspring of a god and a mortal; a typical example of this is furnished by the Dioskouroi who, as their name shows, were sons of Zeus. Their mother was Leda, wife of Tyndareus, king of Sparta, whom Zeus approached in the form of a swan. The founding fathers of various tribes or the founders of cities were also often thought to be the offspring of gods; the Arkadians, for example, believed that their founder was Arkas, son of the Nymph Kallisto and Zeus. Beliefs of this kind are an expression of the ancient Greek tendency to idealise and mythicise the past.

Another category includes heroes who were descended from ancient royal families, who usually themselves became kings. From the house of Pelops, for example, who gave his name to the Peloponnese, sprang the Atreidai, Agamemnon, king of Mycenae, and Menelaos, who became king of Sparta when he married Helen, the daughter of Tyndareus and Leda, mentioned above (the fortunes of these families are bound up with the Trojan War (see pp. 104-137)).

It is unfortunately impossible for us today to establish whether the founding fathers, and the members of the royal families that succeeded them, were historical figures. The episodes associated with them may have been inspired by historical events, but they have passed into history by way of myth, for as they were narrated orally, they were embellished with imaginary features emphasising their significance and value. Myths are impressive precisely because they are based on exaggeration, but this means that their historical value for the modern scholar is very limited.

Today the word hero is usually qualified by the adjective brave, and a heroic action is invariably a good deed demanding a high degree of courage. For Homer, heroes were kings and military leaders, and also ordinary warriors, while in modern times they are soldiers who have lost their lives defending their country. The words 'hero' and 'heroine' are applied to the leading

The Dioskouroi, Kastor and Polydeukes, on horseback, attend their father, Tyndareus, who is seated holding the royal sceptre. (Amphora, c. 520-510 BC. British Museum B 170.)

actors in ancient Greek literature, and also in modern literature, drama and film. though the meaning of the word is different. The modern 'myth-maker' is inspired by social or historical subjects, which he shapes according to the requirements of a scenario and embellishes with completely imaginary elements; his aim is to entertain, and sometimes to educate the viewer or reader, who is consciously distancing himself from his everyday problems and is transported temporarily into an unreal world.

By contrast, the feats of the heroes in the ancient world, as narrated in epic poetry or tragedy, are presented as historical events that unfolded in a heroic age and were incorporated in reality as part of its past. To make it easier to understand the role played by heroes in Greek mythology, reference will be made to a number of specific examples. Attention will be focused initially on two special cases, Herakles and Theseus: the former is a hero of pan-Hellenic character and the latter is associated with ancient myths relating to the history of Athens. Finally, we shall consider the much-discussed Trojan War, because many Greek cities cooperated in this expedition and, regardless of whether it was a historical event or not, it must in ancient times have been an outstanding example of what could be achieved by the united Greek forces.

HERAKLES

Herakles was a very ancient hero who lived many years before the Trojan War, and his feats are often mentioned in Homer's *Odyssey*. His ancestors were from Argos but he was born at Thebes. His mortal father, Amphitryon, was nephew of Elektryon, who at that time was ruler of Mycenae. During a quarrel Amphitryon accidental-ly killed his uncle and was oblig-ed to leave the city, with his wife, Alkmene, and flee to Thebes to seek purification. Here Herakles was born. A hero as powerful as he was, however, had to be giv-en divine origins, and it was therefore said that during Am-phitryon's absence, Zeus himself lay with Alkmene, assuming the form of her husband.

1. The baby Herakles kills the serpents sent by Hera to destroy him. (Stamnos, c. 480 BC. Louvre G 192.)

2. Herakles with a helmet in the form of a lion's head. (Detail from the east pediment of the temple of Aphaia on Aegina, c. 490-480 BC. Munich, Glyptothek 84.)

1

1. Herakles, with the lion's pelt and his club, attempts to steal the Delphic tripod. (Amphora, c. 500-490 BC. Wurzburg, Martin von Wagner Museum 500.)

Zeus's attraction to Alkmene incurred the fatal jealousy of Hera, who decided to destroy the fruit of this love. When Herakles was still an infant she sent two serpents to his cradle to kill him. This episode is depicted on a stamnos in the Louvre Museum (see p. 52): the hero strangles the serpents with his hands, while his brother, Iphikles, flees terrified into the arms of the nurse; next to Herakles stands the goddess Athena, who always protected her favourite hero, and the scene is flanked by Amphitryon and Alkmene who are watching the episode in terror.

Herakles showed that he was no ordinary mortal from a very early age: his divine father had given him special gifts and

2. Herakles, accompanied by Iolaos, shakes hands with his patron goddess, Athena. (Fragment of a krater, c. 420-400 BC. Elis, Archaeological Collection.)

strength. When he grew up he married Megara, the daughter of Kreon, king of Thebes, and had five children by her. Hera, however, who had still not been revenged, drove the hero mad and in his insanity he killed his wife and children.

Crushed by the terrible crime he had committed, Herakles fled to the Delphic oracle to ask Apollo how he could gain expiation. The god advised him to return to his place of origin and place himself at the service of his cousin, Eurystheus, who was at that time king of Mycenae, Tiryns, and Argos. At Hera's urging, Eurystheus attempted to eliminate the hero by assigning him twelve highly dangerous tasks; these, of course, are the 'twelve labours of Herakles'. The first complete depiction of this subject in art adorned the metopes of the temple of Zeus at Olympia. The account of the labours of Herakles that follows is based on the originals and reconstructions of these metopes.

1. The Nemean lion.

2. The Lernaian Hydra.

3. The Stymphalian birds.

4. The Cretan bull.

5. The Keryneian hind.

6. The girdle of the Amazon Hippolyt.

7. The Erymanthian boar.

8. The mares of Diomedes.

9. The cattle of Geryones.

10. The apples of the Hesperides.

11. The mission to Hades.

12. The Augean Stables.

THE LABOURS OF HERAKLES

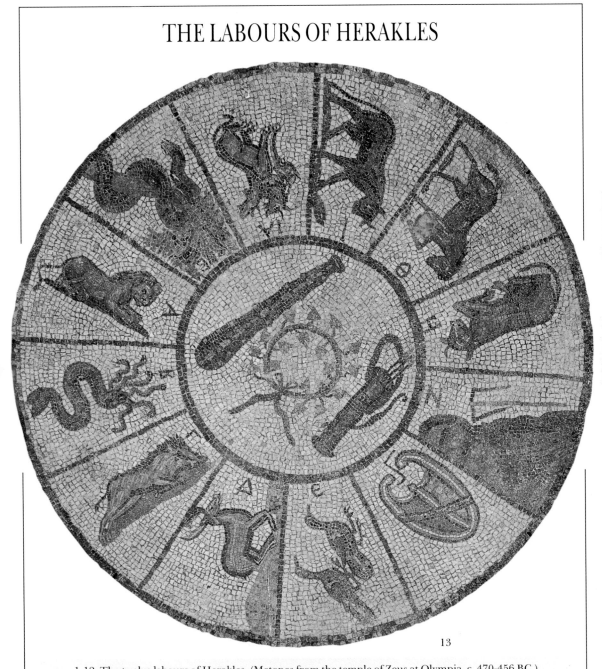

13

1-12. The twelve labours of Herakles. (Metopes from the temple of Zeus at Olympia, c. 470-456 BC.)

13. The opponents of Herakles in his twelve labours. A. The Lion, B. The Lernaian Hydra, C. The Erymanthian boar, D. The Keryneian hind, E. The Stymphalian birds, F. The Girdle of Hippolyta, G. Geryones, H. The Cretan Bull, I. The Mares of Diomedes, J. The Augean Stables, K. Kerberos, L. The dragon guarding the sacred apple-tree in the garden of the Hesperides. In the centre are the hero's weapons. (Part of a mosaic floor from a villa at Elis, middle of the 3rd c. AD. Elis, Archaeological Collection.)

1. THE NEMEAN LION

1. Herakles
wrestles with
the Nemean
lion. (Amphora,
middle of
the 6th c. BC.
Taranto, Museo
Archeologico.)

The inhabitants of the region of Nemea were suffering the destructive attacks of a lion, since they had neglected their duties to the gods. The lion was all-powerful and invincible to human weapons, and Herakles was therefore obliged to wrestle with it hand to hand.

Here the hero is depicted exhausted after killing the beast, and accompanied by his protectress, Athena, and a male figure (Hermes or Iolaos). The trophy won by Herakles from this victory was the lion's pelt, which the hero wore in almost all depictions of him in Greek art.

1

2. Herakles and the Nemean lion. (Metope from the Treasury of the Athenians at Delphi, c. 530-500 BC.)

3. Herakles wrestles with the Nemean lion. The scene is watched by Iolaos and Athena. (Amphora, c. 520 BC. Brescia, Museo Civico.)

2. THE LERNAIAN HYDRA

The Hydra was a monster with snakes springing from its body and breathing fire from its mouth that destroyed men, plants and animals. It lived near Lake Lerna in the area of Argos, where it had been sent by Hera to punish Herakles by tormenting the inhabitants of his place of origin. On the metope from the temple of Zeus at Olympia, the hero is depicted alone as he attempts to cut off the monster's snake heads, which are coiled threateningly around his arms and legs; two more heads took the place of every one that he severed. The depiction on a lekythos in the Louvre Museum (see pp. 62-63)

includes two other elements in the myth: the crab and Iolaos. The crab had emerged from Lake Lerna on the Hydra's orders, in order to help it, and in this scene it bites the hero's foot and hinders his struggles. Iolaos was the faithful companion of Herakles who accompanied him on many of his adventures and made a decisive contribution to this labour: as Herakles cut of the Hydra's heads one by one, Iolaos immediately cauterised the wounds with a torch to prevent them from reduplicating. After his victory, Herakles dipped his arrows in the Hydra's poisonous blood to make them deadly.

1

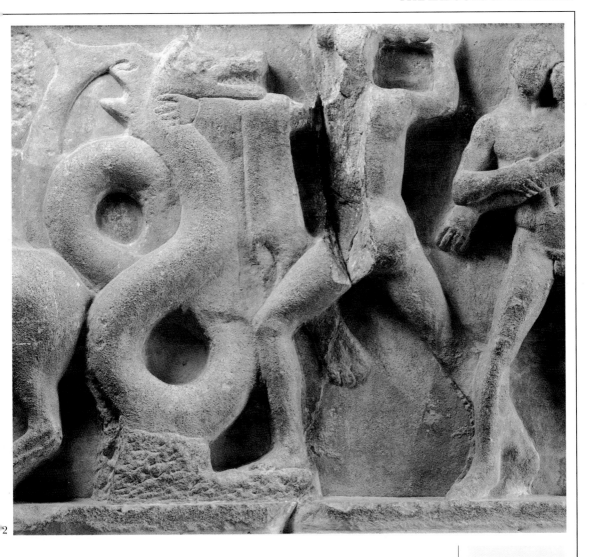

2

2. Herakles and
the Lernaian Hy-
dra. (Frieze slab,
1st c. AD.
Delphi
Museum.)

"The Lernaian Hydra has wrapped itself menacingly around

Herakles' arms and legs. The hero manages to cut off the

heads of the monster with the aid of Iolaos,

who cauterises them one

by one to stop them multiplying."

1

2

3

1-3. Herakles attempts to kill the Lernaian Hydra, while a crab aids the monster by biting his foot. Iolaos helps him to carry out this difficult task, and Athena stands by. (Lekythos, c. 500-490 BC. Louvre CA 598.)

3. THE STYMPHA-LIAN BIRDS

Herakles was also called upon to rid the northern part of Arkadia from the deadly birds that lived in the thick forest near Lake Stymphalia. Tradition has it that these birds were man-eating and had wings as strong as armour. Herakles is shown with the goddess Athena after the end of the struggle; he holds his bow, the weapon he used in this labour, and holds out his other arm as though offering something to the goddess. This gesture and Athena's presence recall the version of the myth according to which the hero caused the birds to fly out of the leaves of the tree by making a loud noise with bronze castanets given to him by the goddess; here, Herakles is either returning the castanets to Athena or offering her some of his victims.

1. Herakles and Athena, after the killing of the Stymphalian birds. (Metope from the temple of Zeus at Olympia, c. 470-456 BC.)

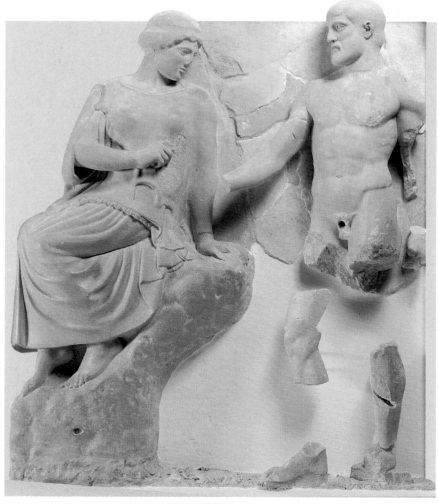

1

The next beast that the hero had to hunt was a bull that lived in Crete near Knossos, where it created terrible havoc. The presence of the bull on Crete is accounted for by two different myths: it was either the animal used by Zeus to transport his beloved Europa to Crete, or the bull by which Pasiphae, the wife of the Cretan king Minos, bore the Minotaur (see pp. 220-223). On this metope, the sculptor depicts the hero threatening the beast with his club, though according to a popular version of the myth, Herakles did not kill the animal but took it alive to Mycenae. Eurystheus was persuaded that Herakles had been successful and set the bull free; after wandering for a long time, the animal came to Marathon where it was finally killed by Theseus (see pp. 95-96).

4. THE CRETAN BULL

2. Herakles subdues the bull of Knossos. (Metope from the temple of Zeus at Olympia, c. 470-456 BC.)

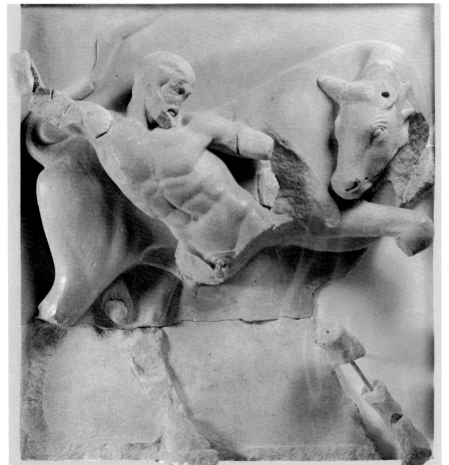

2

5. THE KERYNEIAN HIND

This was a hind dedicated to Artemis with golden horns, which took its name from Mount Keryneia, near Arkadia and Argos, where it lived. Herakles had to catch the animal, which was famous for its fleetness, without wounding it, of course, and bring it alive to Eurystheus. To perform this difficult labour, the hero pursued the hind for many hours, in order to exhaust it, after which he was able to approach it. In the metope the hero has seized the hind by the horns.

1. Herakles and the Keryneian hind. (Metope from the Treasury of the Athenians at Delphi, c. 530-500 BC.)

Eurystheus also asked for the elaborate girdle that had been given by Ares to his daughter, the Amazon queen Hippolyta. Herakles gathered together several companions and set out for the city of Themiskyra, on the Black Sea, where the Amazons dwelt. He was unfortunately unable to carry out his mission, because Hera persuaded the Amazons to attack the strangers. Here we see the outcome of this conflict: Hippolyta, defeated, has fallen to the ground, while Herakles departs with her girdle.

6. THE GIRDLE OF THE AMAZON HIPPOLYTA

2. Herakles and an Amazon. (Frieze slab, 1st c. AD. Delphi Museum.)

2

7. THE ERYMANTHIAN BOAR

1

A wild boar lived on Mount Erymanthos, threatening the inhabitants of Arkadia with destruction. Eurystheus demanded that Herakles should bring this animal alive to Mycenae. To achieve this end, the hero first provoked the animal to chase him and, when it became exhausted after many hours, succeeded in tying it on his shoulders. On the temple Zeus the hero presents the bound boar to Eurystheus who, in terror, has taken refuge inside a jar.

1. The Erymanthian boar. (Part of a mosaic floor from a villa at Elis, middle of the 3rd c. AD. Elis, Archaeological Collection.)

2. Herakles delivers the Erymanthian boar to Eurystheus, who has hidden in a jar, terrified. (Metope from Knossos, c.450 BC.)

2

8. THE MARES OF DIOMEDES

3

Diomedes, the son of the god Ares, was king of Thrace. He was famous for his terrible mares, which he fed with human flesh; this was a kind of punishment that he inflicted on locals or passers-by if they did not obey him. Eurystheus sent Herakles to rid Thrace of this threat and bring the mares alive to Mycenae. One version of the myth relates that the hero tamed the mares after feeding them on their owner, Diomedes. On the metope, Herakles raises his club to subdue one of the wild mares.

3. One of the mares of Diomedes. (Part of a mosaic floor from a villa at Elis, middle of the 3rd c. AD. Elis, Archaeological Collection.)

4. Herakles and the mares of Diomedes. (Frieze slab, 1st c. AD. Delphi Museum.)

4

9. THE CATTLE OF GERYONES

No-one could approach the cattle of the three-bodied Geryones, because they were guarded by Eurytion, son of Ares, and Orthros, a dog with two heads and a serpent's tail. Herakles managed to neutralise the guardians of the herd with his club, and thereafter conquered Geryones himself. Many other adventures of Herakles are associated with this labour, for Geryones lived in the far West, at Erytheia, and during the course of his long journey the hero had to deal with many opponents, proving himself the benefactor of many areas that welcomed him as their guest. On the metope Herakles raises his club in order to destroy the third body of Geryones, while the other two bodies of his monstrous opponent have fallen to the ground.

1. Herakles uses his sword to attack the triple-bodied Geryones. (Amphora, c. 540 BC. Munich, Staatliche Antikensammlungen.)

70

10. THE APPLES OF THE HESPERIDES

The Hesperides lived in a sacred garden which was either in the far West or in the North. In the garden were apple trees that produced golden apples from the fruit that Ga-ia gave Hera as a wedding present. Eurystheus asked Herakles to bring him this sacred fruit, although no-one was allowed to pluck the apples, and Hera had set Ladon, a fearful dragon with

2. Atlas returns with the apples of the Hesperides, while Herakles supports the vault of heaven on his shoulders, with the aid of Athena. (Metope from the temple of Zeus at Olympia, c. 470-456 BC.)

1. Herakles in the garden of the Hesperides. (Hydria, c. 410 BC. British Museum E 244.)

a hundred heads, to guard the garden and protect the fruit. On his way to the garden of the Hesperides, the hero passed by the Caucasus, where Prometheus was bound, and set him free; in return Prometheus told him that his brother, Atlas, would show him the way to the sacred garden. Zeus had sent Atlas to the far West and had made him support the vault of heaven on his shoulders, because Atlas had dared to fight against him in the battle of the Titans. Herakles met the Titan Atlas in the West and agreed to relieve him temporarily of his burden, so that Atlas could fetch the sacred apples for him. What happens next in the myth is the subject of the metope from the temple of Zeus: Athena helps her protege by supporting his burden with her hand, while Atlas has returned with the golden apples and bargains with Herakles, wishing to take the fruit to Eurystheus himself. Herakles, however, managed to deceive Atlas: pretending to agree to the arrangement, he asked Atlas to support the heaven for one more moment, so that he could put some cushions on his shoulders; Atlas agreed, and Herakles at once seized the apples and made off. On a hydria in the British Museum, Herakles sits at his ease in the sacred garden, while the Hesperides pluck the apples to give him; and Ladon is coiled around the trunk of the tree but does not react, since the women have put him to sleep with a magic herb.

11. THE MISSION TO HADES

Eurystheus was dismayed since, despite the fearful difficulties, Herakles had successfully performed all the labours assigned to him. He therefore decided to assign him a virtually impossible task: the capture of Kerberos who guarded the gates of the Underworld. Kerberos was a sinister dog with three heads and serpents springing from various points of his body. No-one had ever succeeded in eluding this terrible monster and escaping from the gloomy kingdom of Hades. Herakles first terrified Charon with his strength and compelled him to take him to the kingdom of Hades; there he met many souls, and also the king and queen of the Underworld themselves,

2. Herakles presents Kerberos to Eurystheus, who has hidden in his jar, terrified. (Caeretan hydria, c. 530-525 BC. Louvre E 701).

2

with whom he discussed his mission. Hades agreed to give Kerberos to him, on condition that he should not use any weapons to capture him. The metope depicts the scene after the struggle: the hero has succeeded in tying up Kerberos and is dragging him off to Mycenae. A hydria in the Louvre depicts the next episode in the myth: Herakles takes the bound Kerberos to Eurystheus's palace and the king, terrified at the sight of the fearsome animal, again seeks refuge inside his jar.

1. Herakles drags the bound Kerberos. (Metope from the temple of Zeus at Olympia, c. 470-456 BC.)

12 THE AUGEAN STABLES

Augeias was king of Elis. His father, Helios, had given him a vast number of flocks and herds; unfortunately, however, the great numbers of animals produced a huge accumulation of dung that threatened the city with pollution and illness. Eurystheus asked Herakles to clean away the dung for Augeias in only a single day. On the metope from the temple of Zeus the hero is depicted shovelling the dung, while the goddess Athena supervises the task. The hero completed this labour very quickly by digging ditches around the fields and collecting the dung in them, after which he diverted the course of two nearby rivers, the Alpheios and the Peneios, which flowed down the ditches and carried away the dung in their streams.

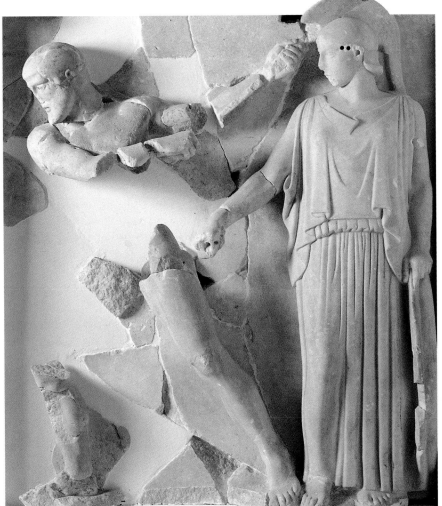

2

2. Herakles cleans the Augean stables. (Metope from the temple of Zeus at Olympia, c. 470-456 BC.)

THE REST OF HERAKLES' LIFE AND HIS DEATH

1.Herakles and his army attack Troy to avenge Laomedon. In the centre is the dominating figure of Athena, supporting her protege. (Reconstruction of the east pediment of the temple of Aphaia on Aegina, c. 490-480 BC. Munich, Glyptothek.)

During the journeys undertaken by Herakles as he carried out his labours he encountered many opponents, whom he had to eliminate in order to continue on his way. These struggles are called 'minor feats' because, although they took place during the course of his labours, they were not carried out on Eurystheus's orders. The hero fought against the Amazons and the Centaurs and took part in the expedition of the Argonauts (see pp. 224-227).

EXPEDITION AGAINST TROY

As he was returning from the Argonaut expedition, Herakles is said to have learned that the king of Troy, Laomedon, was offering his immortal horses – a gift from Zeus to Laomedon's father, Troas, which he had inherited – to anyone who could save his daughter, Hesione. The story began when Zeus punished Poseidon and Apollo for some act of impiety by compelling them to serve Laomedon for one year: the god of the sea undertook to build the walls of Troy, and the god of music was to tend the king's flocks. When they had completed their service, the gods asked Laomedon for the payment they had been promised, but he refused to honour his agreement. In their anger they then decided to take revenge on him: Poseidon sent a sea-monster and Apollo a plague over the city. The Delphic oracle claimed that the disasters would only end if Hesione was sacrificed. Herakles responded to Laomedon's call and managed to rescue Hesione by killing the sea-monster, but the king once more refused to honour his word. The hero gave way at this time, knowing

2. Oineus watches Herakles attack the Centaur Nessos to save his wife, Deianeira. (Stamnos, c. 450-440 BC. British Museum 1896.7-16.5)

that one day he would have his revenge. The opportunity arose when he was returning from Themiskyra, where he had been sent by Eurystheus to fetch the girdle of the Amazon Hippolyta; with the support of his comrades, Herakles killed Laomedon and his family, apart from Hesione, whom he gave to his friend Telamon, and Laomedon's youngest son, Priam, who later became king of Troy.

HERAKLES AND DEIANEIRA

After Herakles had completed his service with Eurystheus, he decided to start a new life. When Herakles went down to Hades to fetch Kerberos, he had met Meleager, who asked him to go to

1. Herakles and Deianeira, with Hyllos in her arms, together with Athena and Oineus. (Pelike, c. 480-470 BC Louvre G 229.)

2. Apollo chases Herakles who is trying to make off with the sacred tripod of Delphi. The episode is watched by Athena and Artemis. (Amphora, 520 BC. Berlin, Staatliche Museen F 2159.)

Kalydon and ask his father, king Oineus, for the hand of his sister, Deianeira. When he arrived in Kalydon, Herakles found that he had been preceded by the river god Acheloos, who was insisting on marrying Deianeira against her will. Urged on by the bride herself, the hero wrestled with the river god and defeated him, thus successfully fulfilling the promise he had given to the soul of Meleager. After the wedding ceremony the newly married couple set off for Tiryns. On their way they had to cross the river Euenos, where the Centaur Nessos lived; like all the other Centaurs, he had the form of a man from the waist up and a horse from the waist down. Nessos took Deianeira in his arms on the pretext that the gods had assigned to him the task of carrying travellers from one bank of the river to the other; but half way across he began to make love to her and the woman screamed to warn her husband (see p. 77). Herakles then fired one of his arrows, tipped with the poisonous blood of the Lernaian Hydra, and fatally wounded the Centaur. Nessos made sure he had his revenge, however. Just before he died he told Deianeira that his blood had aphrodisiac properties and urged her to gather it, as it ran from his wound, and keep it away from the light of the sun.

For several years Herakles and Deianeira, together with their son Hyllos, lived happily at Tiryns. On a pelike in the Louvre, the hero is depicted as a family head: although he is holding the lion's pelt, bow and club, he is not naked as usual, but

2

wears a himation; Hyllos, in his mother's arms, reaches out his hands to touch his father, and the happy family is flanked by Oineus and Athena. The event that marked the beginning of the end of Herakles' family bliss was his decision to take part in an archery contest organised by Eurytos, king of Oichalia (the precise location of which has not been established), the prize for the victor being his daughter, Iole. As was to be expected, the hero excelled in the competition, but the king refused to honour his promise, because the victor was already married and therefore could not take Iole as his lawful wife. In his anger, Herakles stole the horses of Eurytos and returned to Tiryns. Shortly afterwards, he

3

3. Herakles and Triton. One of the opponents encountered by the hero on his journeys was the sea-god Triton, son of Poseidon and Amphitrite. (Amphora, c. 520-510 BC. British Museum B 223.)

was visited there by Iphitos who demanded his father's horses; Herakles killed him, however. Once again the hero had to flee his country in order to seek expiation. When he came to the Delphic oracle to consult Apollo, the Pythia refused to answer him, because he bore the pollution of a murder committed in violation of the rules of hospitality. The Pythia's answer enraged Herakles even more, and he snatched the sacred tripod of Apollo from the sanctuary with the aim of founding his own oracle at Pheneos.

This was the cause of the fearful conflict that broke out between Apollo and Herakles, which was resolved only after Zeus intervened and threw a thunderbolt between them. In the end, Herakles and his family fled to Trachis, where he was the guest of king Keyx.

Trachis is the setting of Sophocles' tragedy the *Trachinian Women*, which is the first full narrative of the events leading to Herakles' death. The tragedy begins with Deianeira announcing that her husband has been away for three years and three months, and noting that the Delphic oracle had predicted that after this period Herakles would either die or would be redeemed. Alarmed, she sends her son, Hyllos, to look for his father. She soon learns from a messenger that her husband had received instructions from Zeus to serve queen Omphale (probably in

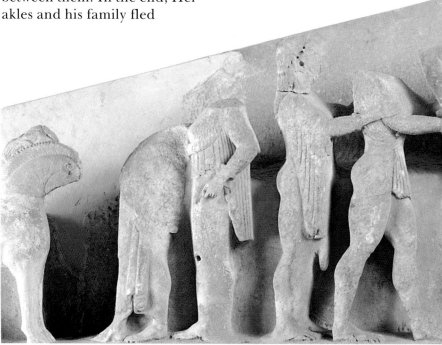

Lydia) in order to expiate the murder of Iphitos. After this he had conquered and destroyed Oichalia and had taken Iole as his servant, and had already sent her to Trachis. Although the messenger does not reveal to Deianeira that Herakles' expedition against Oichalia had amorous motives, she quickly learns the truth, and decides to use the love potion given to her by the Centaur Nessos before he died, so that she could again win the love of her husband. She chooses an elegant cloak and smears it with the magical fluid, before handing it to the messenger, with instructions to give it to Herakles himself and

to keep it away from the light of the sun until her husband put it on. The queen realises her tragic mistake after the messenger has already departed: the gift of a man who had fallen victim to her husband's strength could bode no good. Meanwhile, Herakles delightedly puts on his wife's present, but the garment immediately clings to his skin and causes him terrible pain. Hyllos returns to Trachis, tells his mother what has happened and blames her for it. Deianeira then leaves the palace and puts an end to her own life, whereupon Hyllos learns his mother's real intentions and realises that he has accused her unjustly. He then tells his father, who realises that he has come to the end of his life; he asks Hyllos to take him to the top of Mount

The struggle between Herakles and Apollo for the Delphic tripod. (East pediment of the Treasury of the Siphnians at Delphi, c. 530 BC.)

Oite and burn his body on a large pyre to free him from the pain. Hyllos, overwhelmed with grief, is persuaded to carry out his father's instructions, but at the last minute cannot bring himself to set fire to the pyre; the hero Philoktetes then appears, and is persuaded to contribute to the redeeming of the hero, in return for which Herakles gives him his bow and arrows. The end of the myth is known from other sources: the goddess Athena descends in her chariot, raises Herakles from the pyre and takes him with her to Mount Olympos, where he is welcomed by the gods. Herakles is rewarded for his feats by a place amongst the twelve gods of Olympos, becomes immortal, and marries Hebe (the goddess of youth) who gives him the gift of eternal youth. The wedding of Herakles and Hebe is depicted on a kylix in the Berlin Museum: the couple are led by Apollo and Hermes, while Hestia and the Hours pour libations in their honour; on the other side of the vase, which is pre-

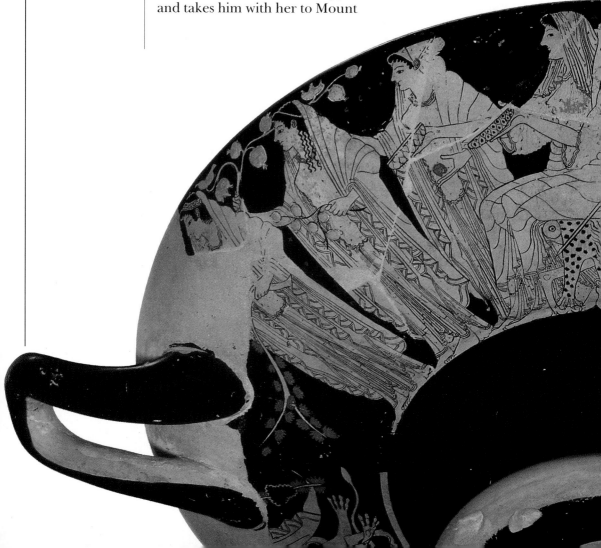

served in fragments, are depicted Zeus and Hera, Poseidon and Amphitrite, Ares and Aphrodite, Dionysos and Ariadne, and Iris.

Eurystheus continued to persecute Herakles' house, however: he banned his descendants from the Argolid and forbade them to enter Boeotia. In Euripides' tragedy *The Herakleidai*, the children of Herakles seek protection from Theseus in Athens, as a result of which the Argives marched against Attica; the Athenians and the Herakleidai routed their opponents and Hyllos killed the fiend Eurystheus. The positive outcome of the battle opened the way for the return of the Herakleidai to the Peloponnese, but the Delphic oracle predicted that it was only the third generation of descendants of the pan-Hellenic hero that would rule in his place of origin; for the next sixty years, therefore, the Argolid was ruled by the family of Atreus, the brother of Eurystheus's wife, until it was exterminated after the Trojan War.

Apollo and Hermes accompany Herakles and Hebe to Olympos, while Hestia and the Hours honour them with libations. (Kylix, c. 500 BC. Berlin, Staatliche Museen F 2278.)

ATTIC MYTHS AND THESEUS

THE ORIGINS OF THE ATHENIANS
AND THEIR EARLIEST KINGS

The traditional accounts of the foundation of Athens state that the Athenians were descended from Kekrops, who was an offspring of the Attic soil. This belief was frequently sung by Attic authors and artists, who took every opportunity to stress proudly that the Athenians differed from the rest of the Greeks in being indigenous. In art the origins of Kekrops are in-dicated in the manner he is depicted, with the form of a man from the waist up and of a serpent from the waist down; his association with a chthonic being like the serpent, which is in continual contact with the earth, is a clear allusion to his origins. Kekrops was the earliest king of Athens and had a wife Aglauros, who bore him four children: Erysichthon, Aglauros, Herse and Pandrosos. Kekrops is said to have instituted marriage and burial and to have organised all the independent demes of Attica into a kind of federal state. During his reign, Athena and Poseidon competed for the title of official patron of the city. The contest was judged on the basis of the gifts offered by the two gods, and the decision was taken either by Kekrops alone or by a council of gods in which the king himself naturally took part. This episode is depicted on a hydria in the Hermitage Museum: the olive tree that grew when Athena struck the rock of the Acropolis with her spear is depicted between the two rivals; at the right Poseidon holds the reigns of a horse in one hand and with the other raises his trident in order to strike the rock and cause the spring to gush forth. The snake, which slithers at the feet of the gods, probably symbolised the chthonic origins of the Athenians. and the small figure of Nike flying between them holds her arms towards Athena as though pronouncing the outcome of the contest. In the end Athena's gift was preferred over the offering from Poseidon, because the olive was an omen of peace and prosperity for the city,

Kekrops, the first indigenous king of Athens, together with Hephaistos and Herse, watches Gaia handing the new-born Erichthonios to Athena. (Kylix, c. 430 BC. Berlin, Staatliche Museen F 2537.)

1. Athena competes with Poseidon for the official patronage of the city of Athens. (Drawing from the decoration of a hydria, c.400-350 BC. Hermitage Museum KAB 6a.)

1

unlike water which was to be found in abundance around the Attic peninsula, and the horse which was regarded as an animal of war. Since that time Athena has continued to act as patron and benefactor of her city. In a scene on a skyphos in the Louvre Museum the goddess contributes to the building of the walls of Athens by leading a Giant who is carrying a huge rock. Athena is also connected with Erichthonios, one of the earliest kings of the city. Erichthonios is said to have been born from the seed of Hephaistos that fell on the earth when the virgin Athena rejected his amorous advances. On a kylix in Berlin, Gaia hands the newborn infant to Athena; the figure at the left with the serpent's body is, of course, Kekrops, and the scene is completed at the right by Hephaistos and Herse, a reference to the ending of this myth. Athena loved Erichthonios and brought him up as though he were her actual child; at one point she put him in a box with two snakes for his protection, and entrusted the box to the daughters of Kekrops with instructions always to keep it closed. Overcome by their curiosity, however, they opened it, were driven insane by what they saw, and jumped from the Acropolis rock.

When Erichthonios ascended to the throne of Athens he paid special honour to Athena who had brought him up; he devoted a xoanon (a wooden statue) of her on the Acropolis and, according to the myth, it was he who established the festival of the Panathenaia in her honour. Erichthonios was succeeded by his son, Pandion, and he in turn by his son, Erechtheus. His descendants, the Erectheids, ruled Athens for several generations, after which the throne passed to the children of Theseus, the Theseids. The recurrence of the compound *chthon,* meaning earth, in the name of some of the kings (Erysichthon, Erichthonios, and Erechtheus) is an allusion to their indigenous origins. This list of the successive kings, of course, has no histori-

cal value for modern research, but the authority enjoyed by these myths in antiquity should not be underestimated; they formed the connecting link between the historical period and the glorious past of Athens, and consolidated the view that the Athenians were derived from their indigenous kings, and were thus born and bred on Attic soil.

INTERPRETATION

Beginning in the 6th century BC, Athens gradually developed into an important power in the Greek world. In 594-593 BC Solon became archon and passed his legislation. At the end of the 6th century, the tyranny

2. A Giant, accompanied by Athena, carries an enormous rock to build the walls of Athens. (Skyphos, c. 440-430 BC. Louvre G.372.)

2

of Peisistratos was abolished. In 508-507 BC, the archon Kleisthenes organised the inhabitants of Attica into ten tribes. Athens made an important contribution to checking the Persian forces, who were defeated at the battle of Marathon (490 BC) and the naval battle of Salamis (480 BC). To protect the Greek cities from the Persian threat, the Athenians organised the Delian Confederacy, which established Athens as a powerful force in Greece. The history of the city was directly linked with its mythical past. The reforms of Kleisthenes (508-507 BC) were sealed by the Delphic oracle, which chose ten Attic heroes to give their names to the ten tribes. Furthermore, one tradition has it that two of the major Greek peoples were descended from Athenians; Xouthos, the son of Hellen, fled from Thessaly to Attica. There he married Kreousa, the daughter of king Erechtheus, and had two sons, Ion and Achaios, who became the founding fathers of the Ionians and the Achaians

An excellent example of the influence enjoyed by myths in historical Athens is provided by Euripides' tragedy *Ion* (413 BC), in which the poet claims that Apollo was the real father of Ion. Thus, at the very period that the Athenians were trying to retain their influence over Ionia, the tradition was created that the founding father of the Ionians was the son of a god and an indigenous Athenian woman: this can hardly have been mere coincidence.

The greater the power of Athens grew, the more the links with her mythical past were stressed. The message that the city had taken and continued to take the lead was strongly expressed in the art and literature of Classical Athens. The talents and feats of Theseus, the supreme Athenian hero and king. rival the multi-faceted personality of the pan-Hellenic hero Herakles. We shall return to this theme at the end of this chapter, having first examined in detail the myths relating to Theseus.

Seven of the ten eponymous heroes of Attica: Demophon, Oineus, Klymenos, Philoktetes, Akamas, Hippothon and Antiochos. (Hydria, c. 410 BC. British Museum E 224.)

Theseus wrestles
with Kerkyon.

THE LABOURS OF THESEUS
(Kylix, c. 440-430 BC.
British Museum E 84.)

Theseus attacks the
pig of Krommyon,
while the old woman
Phaia attempts to
obstruct him.

Theseus ties Sines, the Pine-bender,
to pine trees.

Theseus holds Prokroustes' hammer and compels the robber to lie down on one of his beds.

Theseus brings the dead body of the Mino- taur from the gate of the Labyrinth.

Theseus throws away Skiron's bowl, as the robber falls from the cliff up which the man-eat- ing turtle is climbing.

Theseus kills the bull of Marathon.

THESEUS

THE BIRTH OF THESEUS

When Aigeus became king of Athens, he visited the Delphic oracle to learn the reason why he had not yet acquired any successors. The Pythia, as always, gave him an enigmatic reply: 'Do not open the mouth of the wine-flask until you reach Athens.' Aigeus was unable to interpret the oracle, and therefore decided, before returning to Athens, to go to Troizen to consult king Pittheus, who was famous for his wisdom. Pittheus understood the meaning of Pythia's words and decided to exploit the situation to strengthen the links between Troizen and Athens. He is said to have convinced Aigeus, either by making him drunk, or through persuasion, to spend the night with his daughter, Aithra, who in the end brought him the successor he desired. Before he departed, Aigeus concealed his sandals and sword beneath a rock and told Aithra that if she bore a son she was to reveal the hiding place to him when he grew up. If he had the strength to raise the rock on his own, she was to send him to Athens with the sandals and sword, so that Aigeus would be able to recognise him. Aigeus then returned to Athens and Aithra bore Theseus nine months later. It was not enough, however, for a hero of this stature to be the offspring of royal families; his bravery transcended human bounds, and therefore tradition tells us that Aithra had coupled with Poseidon before she lay with Aigeus, and the god of the sea was therefore recognised as the hero's heavenly father. When Theseus grew to manhood, he raised the rock and found the things concealed there by his father, took them, and set out on his journey to meet him.

1. Theseus lifts the rock and finds his father's sword and sandals. Aithra watches her son proudly. (Clay tablet, 1st c. AD. British Museum D 594.)

2. Theseus and Skiron. (Metope from the Treasury of the Athenians at Delphi, c. 530-500 BC.)

2

THE LABOURS OF THESEUS

On his way from Troizen to Athens, the young Theseus encountered robbers and evildoers who were threatening the safety of travellers, wrestled with them, and finally killed them using their own weapons (see pp. 90-91). First, as he crossed from Epidauros, he met Periphetes, who killed passers-by with an iron club; Theseus, destroyed the villain and kept his club. At Kenchreai (a harbour of Corinth) lurked Sines, called the Pine-bender, because he used to tie passers-by to two trees that he bent over, which he then released so that they tore their bodies apart. At Krommyon (modern Ayioi Theodoroi near Corinth) lived a pig that caused great destruction; the animal was protected by an old woman called Phaia, who tried to persuade the hero to take pity on it, but he attacked it with stones and ultimately managed to kill it with his sword. When Theseus came to the Skironian Rocks (modern Kakia Skala) he found himself face to face with the robber Skiron, who compelled his victims to wash his feet and, as they stooped, pushed them off the rock so that they fell into the sea, where they were devoured by a turtle; the hero killed Skiron in the same way. After this Theseus won a wrestling match with Kerkyon, who killed passers-by on the way from Eleusis, compelling them to wrestle with him. Finally, at some point of the Sacred Way, which linked Eleusis with Athens, there lived Prokroustes; he made passers-by lie down on a bed which was either too long or too short, depending on their height. He then killed them all by stretching the bodies of the short ones until they were long enough for the bed, and cutting off the extremities of the tall ones that stuck out from it. Prokroustes met the same fate as his victims, and after all these adventures, Theseus came victorious to Athens. This event is represented in the scene on an amphora in the British Museum, in which Aigeus shakes the hand of his son, while Aithra bids him farewell and his heavenly father, Poseidon, looks on.

1. Theseus and Ariadne. (Oinochoe, 7th c. BC. Herakleion Museum.)

2. Poseidon watches Aithra bidding farewell to Theseus and Aigeus welcoming him. (Amphora, c. 470-460 BC. British Museum E 264.)

1

2

As we have seen already, these labours of Theseus took place during his journey from Troizen to Athens, and they therefore probably symbolise the transition of the hero from his childhood, which he passed at Troizen, to the mature phase of his life, which is associated with Athens, of which he later became king. On a metope of the Treasury of the Siphnians at Delphi, Theseus is presented, triumphant, to the goddess Athena, who welcomes him to her city. Nev-

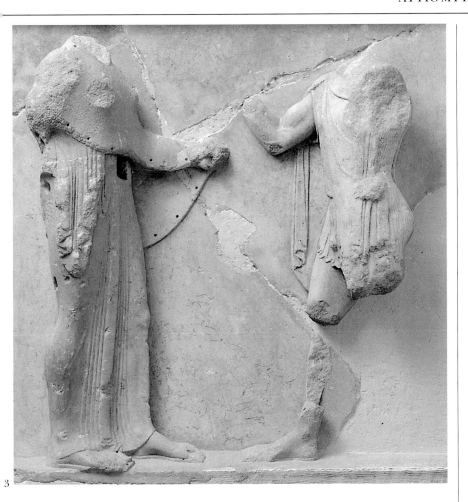

3

3. Theseus and the bull of Marathon. (Metope from the Treasury of the Athenians at Delphi, c. 530-500 BC.)

ertheless, Theseus had to undergo other trials before he was ultimately recognised by his father. When the hero arrived at Athens, Aigeus had married Medea, a demoniacal woman who had killed her own children out of jealousy of her previous husband, Jason (see pp. 238-239). She immediately recognised Theseus, even before Aigeus had realised that the stranger who had come to the city was really his son. Realising that his arrival would affect their marriage, she devised a plan to eliminate him: she persuaded Aigeus to test the 'stranger' by asking him to kill the terrible bull that was wreaking havoc at Marathon (probably the same animal that Herakles had caught on Crete, see p. 65). The hero, however, did not succumb to this opponent, either, but managed to kill the fearsome animal and spare Marathon from the destruction it was causing. Medea was disappointed at the failure of her design, but did not

1. Theseus and the bull of Marathon. (Metope from the Treasury of the Athenians at Delphi, c. 530-500 BC.)

give up; she at once prepared a poison, which she intended to offer to their guest during the banquet to be given in his honour. At the last moment, however, Theseus produced his father's symbols (the sword and sandals) and Aigeus recognised him, welcomed his son joyfully to the palace, and punished his cunning wife with exile. The recognition of Theseus by his father dismayed Aigeus's brother, Pallas, and his fifty sons, who believed that Aigeus had no successors and hoped that one day they would rightfully claim the throne of Athens. They therefore decided to use force to get rid of the newcomer who was to deprive them of power. The resulting conflict, however, which took place at Pallene, ended in Theseus's favour, who once more, overcame his opponents. As a result of all his successes,

Theseus was proclaimed the rightful successor of his father to the throne of Athens. His problems were not yet over, however; that year the Athenians had to send seven young men and seven girls to Crete to be given as food to the Minotaur. The Minotaur was a monster with the head of a bull and the body of a man, who had been born from the union of Pasiphae, the queen of Crete, and the bull sent by Poseidon to the island (possibly the same animal brought by Herakles to Mycenae, which Theseus had killed at Marathon). The sacrifice of the fourteen Athenian youths was a kind of tax, which Athens was obliged to pay every nine years to Minos, the king of Crete, to appease him for the death of his son, who had been killed in Attica. Theseus decided to go to Crete himself in order to free his city from this terrible obligation. The ship with the young men and women set out from Athens with black sails. It had been agreed that if the mission was successful and the young people were saved, the ship should return with white sails hanging from its masts. An important contribution to their success was made by the daughter of Minos, Ariadne, who was captivated by Theseus and decided to help him. The Minotaur was shut up in the labyrinth, a vast area with many corridors and passages, in which anyone who entered got lost, be-

2

cause it was impossible to find the exit. Theseus overcame this obstacle with the help of Ariadne, who gave him a ball of thread, having first tied the end of the thread to the entrance to the labyrinth. As the hero penetrated deep into the labyrinth, he gradually unwound the ball of wool, and having successfully killed the Minotaur, he had only to rewind the ball in order to return to the light of day.

The triumphant Athenians boarded their ship and set off on the return journey. With them

2-3. The Minotaur and a stylised labyrinth. (Silver coin from Knossos, 5th c. BC.)

3

1

1. Steatite rhyton in the shape of a bull's head. (From the Little Palace at Knossos, c. 1550-1500 BC. Herakleion Museum.)

2. Theseus wrestles with the Minotaur. (Vase, 6th c. BC. Herakleion Museum.)

went Ariadne, because Theseus had promised that he would make her his wife. During the voyage they stopped at the island of Naxos, where the beautiful Ariadne attracted the attention of the god Dionysos; then Athena intervened and advised the hero to leave his beloved on the island, because, of course, it would not be sensible to oppose the desires of a god. The Athenians also put in at Delos, where they offered sacrifices to Apollo and, clasping each other's hands danced the *geranos*, a dance whose movements mimic their wanderings inside the labyrinth. This episode is depicted on the neck of the François vase in Florence, on which the young Athenian men and women are dancing their way onto their ship (see pp. 100-101). Unhappily, however, because of their enthusiasm and the festivities, they forgot to raise the white sails. When Aigeus saw the ship returning from afar with black sails, he believed that his son had died and in his despair threw himself off the rock on which he stood and was killed. Since that time the sea which received the unhappy father has been called the Aegean Sea.

Theseus was distressed when he was told about the pointless death of his father, but soon had to assume his duties. Having been officially proclaimed king of the city, he married Phaidra, who gave him two sons, Akamas and Demophon. His most important task, while he was ruler of Athens, was the unification of all the settlements of Attica into one 'state' with a single government, and the establishment of the festival of the *Synoikia*, ('Unification') in commemoration of this event. He also defeated the

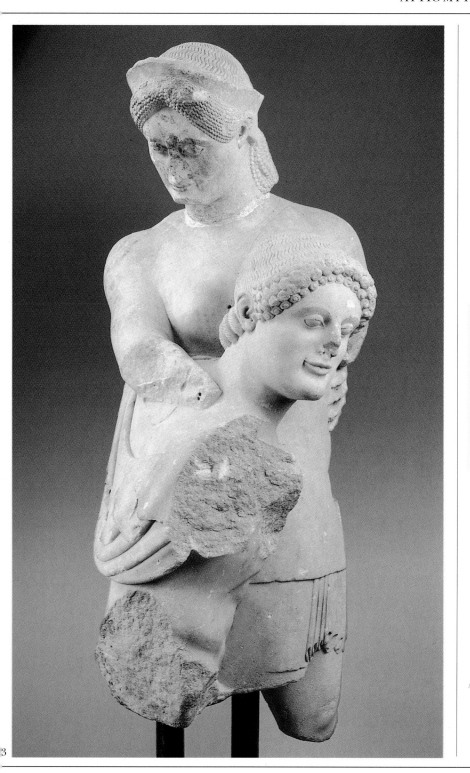

3. Theseus abducts the Amazon Antiope. (Pediment from the temple of Apollo at Eretria, c. 510 BC. Eretria Museum.)

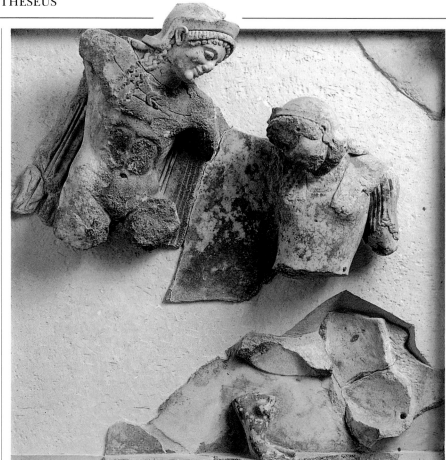

1. Theseus and an Amazon. (One of the south metopes from of the Treasury of the Athenians at Delphi, c. 530-500 BC.)

army of Amazons that appeared outside his city (see pp. 212-215); and he fought on the side of his close friend Peirithoos, king of the Lapiths in Thessaly, when the Centaurs invaded his wedding feast (see pp. 232-235).

The hero's death is associated with a story that probably took place when his wife was no longer alive. Theseus and Peirithoos decided that, because of their courage and their origins, they ought to marry women worthy of them. Theseus desired the 'fair Helen', and with the assistance of his friend he carried her off from the palace of her father, Tyndareus, at Sparta. Helen's brothers, the Dioskouroi, who were also very strong because they were the children of Zeus, managed to rescue her, however, and took revenge on Theseus by compelling his mother, Aithra, to enter their sister's service. Aithra followed Helen to Troy as her servant, where she was to be saved by her grandchildren, Akamas and Demophon.

Peirithoos was even bolder, and wanted to win Persephone, the wife of Hades, and the two heroes were therefore obliged to go down to the Underworld. Hades, however, who was aware of their intentions, deceived them; he pretended to make them welcome and offered them two luxurious thrones to sit on.

The heroes accepted his hospitality, but the god pinned them forever to these seats and thus punished them for their impiety. According to one view, Theseus never returned from Hades and died in this way. Other myths say that when Herakles descended to the Underworld in order to capture Kerberos, he met the two heroes, but succeeded in freeing only Theseus, who when he returned to Athens found Menestheus on the throne and was obliged to leave the city. Finally, others put the descent to Hades amongst the youthful adventures of the hero and others state that towards the end of his life, Theseus decided to abdicate voluntarily. According to these last two versions of the myth, the hero died on Skyros at the hands of the king Lykomedes, who pushed him from a rock. In 475 BC, Kimon brought back the bones of Theseus from Skyros to Athens and placed them in a heroon (the Theseion) which had been built in his honour.

2. Athenian men and women dance the geranos, as they embark on their ship at Delos. (Volute krater, c. 570 BC. Florence 4209.)

2

THESEUS
AND
HERAKLES

The myths concerning Herakles and Theseus have many points in common, but also some important differences. One basic point of similarity between the two heroes is their divine origin, which gives them superhuman powers; they successfully deal with many different kinds of monstrous beings, such as the Lernaian Hydra and the Minotaur or the Cretan bull and the bull of Marathon. They could be described as benefactors, since they rid the ancient world of various elements that threatened the social order and prosperity.

Despite this, however, their motives, and their characters, were radically different. Herakles was by nature wilder and had a quicker temper; he killed his own family and committed several pointless murders, of which even the Delphic oracle refused to purify him (such as when he exterminated the family of Eurytos because of his amorous desire for Iole). Herakles wandered the entire world to carry out his labours and in the end did not settle in any one place. Indeed,

three different areas of Greece lay claim to him: the Argolid, which was his place of origin, Boeotia, where he was born, and Aetolia, the home of his wife, Deianeira. According to the myth, his troubled life was due to the grudge borne by Hera against his mother, Alkmene. This was the account given by the myth-makers to delineate the personality of a hero who travelled from one end of the world to the other, and whose feats were known throughout the length and breadth of Greece.

In contrast, Theseus, once he had grown to manhood, was directly connected with only one city, Athens, in which he lived and over which he ruled. Furthermore, he carried out his labours of his own free will and not as a result of compulsory service to another. He seems to be more pacific by nature, since he does not cause conflict (compare the seizure of the Delphic tripod by Herakles), but for the most part takes only defensive action to protect his city and his rights. Theseus is not only a mighty warrior, but also concerns him-

Herakles attacks Geras, the personification of old age. (Amphora, c. 470 BC British Museum E 290.)

self with the political affairs of his country (the *Synoikia*) and was the model of the king who worked indefatigably for the security and prosperity of his land.

Ultimately, however, Herakles defeats death, whereas Theseus dies, meeting an inglorious death for a hero like himself. The view has been advanced that the labours of Herakles symbolise the struggle against death; this interpretation seems probably enough, when one considers that the hero descended to the Underworld and returned to earth with the fearful Kerberos, while Theseus only managed to return from his journey there with the aid of Herakles. Herakles' indefatigable struggle for life is suggested by a scene on an amphora in the British Museum, in which the hero is using his club to pursue Geras, the personification of old age. Through his adventures and the torment that marked his life on earth, Herakles secured a place in Mount Olympos, and immortality and eternal youth, while Theseus died like any mortal, despite being honoured as a hero.

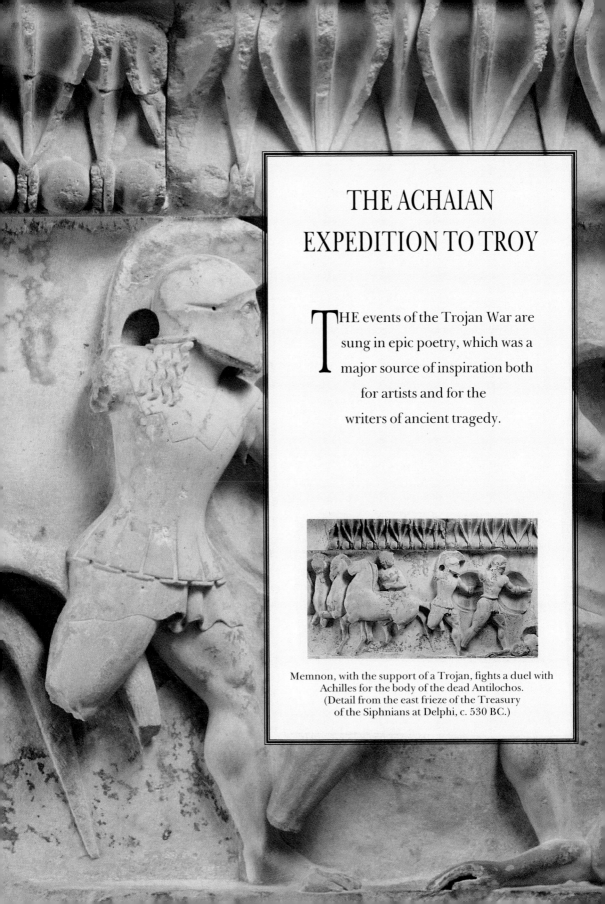

THE ACHAIAN
EXPEDITION TO TROY

T HE events of the Trojan War are
sung in epic poetry, which was a
major source of inspiration both
for artists and for the
writers of ancient tragedy.

Memnon, with the support of a Trojan, fights a duel with
Achilles for the body of the dead Antilochos.
(Detail from the east frieze of the Treasury
of the Siphnians at Delphi, c. 530 BC.)

THE CAUSES OF THE WAR

According to the epic tradition, the cause of the war was the protest by Gaia at the remorseless increase in the human population; the goddess suffered greatly from the weight of her burden, and complained to Zeus. The father of the gods, noting the need to reduce the number of people on the earth, caused the war. The expedition against Troy, like many other long bloody conflicts was, according to Hesiod, the reason for the extermination of the race of heroes. The immediate cause of the war was the abduction of the 'fair Helen' by Paris. The son of the king of Troy visited the palace of Menelaos at Sparta, where he was welcomed with appropriate honours; his purpose, however, was to carry off the beautiful wife of the master of the house and take her to his homeland, in order to make her his own wife. How did this story begin, however? What force impelled Paris to violate the institutions of marriage and hospitality and ignore the terrible consequences that such an act of impiety might incur?

It all began at the wedding of Peleus and Thetis. Thetis was one of the daughters of Nereus, and had enchanted both Zeus and Poseidon with her beauty; a major conflict would have broken out between the two gods had not Themis, the goddess of Justice, come between them, and warned them that, if Thetis coupled with a god, she was destined to produce a son who would surpass his father and overthrow the existing balance in the world, which had been consolidated after so many struggles. The gods immediately saw reason and decided to marry Thetis to Peleus, a brave young man who ruled on Mount Pelion, where he had been sent by

1-2. The procession of gods at the wedding of Peleus and Thetis. (Volute krater, c. 570 BC, Florence 4209.)

his father Aiakos, the king of Aegina. It was decided that Peleus would have to capture the Nereid in order to demonstrate that he was worthy of marrying a goddess. The hero called upon all his powers, for Thetis was indomitable and always managed to escape her opponents by changing form. One night at full moon, when the Nereid was dancing with her sisters on the shore, Peleus suddenly appeared before her and held her tightly in his arms; the girl began to change form, now into a snake, now a dragon and now a lion, but Peleus did not let her out of his arms for a moment until Thetis became exhausted and surrendered to him.

The marriage of a goddess to a mortal was a major event, and all the gods honoured the imposing ceremony with their presence, offering gifts and prayers to the newly-weds. There is an impressive depiction of the myth on the François Vase in Florence, in which Thetis is seated in her new home, while Peleus stands before the door and welcomes the guests; the first to greet the

3

groom are the wise Centaur Cheiron, Iris, Hestia, Chariklo (the wife of Cheiron) Demeter and Dionysos, who carries his wedding present, a gold amphora full of wine; they are followed by the three Hours, and Zeus with Hera riding on their chariot and accompanied by two of the Muses, Ourania and Kalliope, with four more of the Muses, Melpomene, Kleio, Euterpe and Thaleia, walking behind them; Poseidon and Amphitrite, and Ares and Aphrodite also arrive

3. Peleus attempts to seize Thetis, who transforms herself into a serpent to escape. (Epinetron, 425-420 BC. Athens, National Archaeological Museum 1629.)

2

on chariots, with the Muses Stesichore, Erato and Polymnia on foot; Apollo, accompanied by Leto, drives his four-horsed chariot, with the three Graces; next to them; the chariot of Athena and Artemis is welcomed by the parents of the bride, Nereus and Doris, while the driver of the following chariot is Hermes, accompanied by his mother, Maia; next to them stand the three Fates with their mother, Themis; in the last chariot are Okeanos and Tethys (the parents of Doris), while the women walking next to them are probably the Nereids, the bride's sisters; finally, the procession is completed by Hephaistos and the sea-god Triton.

Although no deity should have been missing from such an important event, Eris, the goddess of strife, had not been invited for obvious reasons. She naturally became aware of the festivities and decided to take her revenge for the insult offered her by causing a dispute which would have deadly consequences. She ap-

Hermes takes Athena, Hera and Aphrodite to Paris, who is playing the lyre as the grazes his flocks. (Kylix, c. 490-480 BC. Berlin, Staatliche Museen F 2291.)

peared at the wedding feast and offered a golden apple for the most beautiful goddess; her challenge was taken up by Aphrodite, Athena and Hera, who began to argue with each other about who was the most beautiful. Zeus intervened to put an end to the dispute and appointed Paris-Alexander as judge, ordering Hermes to take the three goddesses to him. Paris's father was Priam, the youngest son of Laomedon, and the only one who survived after Herakles laid siege to Troy. Priam had restored his father's kingdom and ruled together with his wife, Hekabe, and their children Hektor, Kassandra, Paris, Troilos, Polyxene and Deiphobos. The first signs of the impending disaster came when Hekabe was pregnant with Paris and dreamed that she had given birth to a torch that set fire to Troy and consumed it. As soon as their son was born, the two terrified parents gave him to a shepherd with orders to kill him, but the shepherd took pity on him and brought him up. Paris grew up into a handsome, intrepid young man, and was therefore given the name Alexander. He lived in the mountains of Troy graz-

NEMESIS   TYCHE   PEITHO   HELEN   APHRODITE

Aphrodite and her followers attempt to persuade the 'fair Helen' to follow Paris to Troy. (Amphoriskos, c. 430-420 BC. Berlin Staatliche Museen 30036.)

ing his herds, but later fate drew him to his real father, who recognised him.

Hermes took the three goddesses to the grazing grounds of Troy to meet Paris, but as soon as he found himself in their majestic presence he was so terrified that he ran to hide. Hermes reassured him however and revealed Zeus's orders to him. The goddesses approached him and tried to tempt him, not only with their beauty, but also with their gifts: Athena promised him strength and invincibility, Hera the kingdom of Asia and Europe, and Aphrodite the most beautiful woman in the world. When Paris gazed upon the goddess of love, he was unable to resist her allure and yielded to temptation.

His decision took him to Sparta, to the palace of Menelaos, the husband of the 'fair Helen'. In order to satisfy the desire planted in his heart by Aphrodite, the hero had to win the most beautiful woman in the world and make her his wife. The scene adorning an amphoriskos in Berlin is very interesting: Helen sits on Aphrodite's lap and listens carefully to her instructions; next to them stands Peitho, symbolising the ultimate surrender of Menelaos's wife to the persuasive words of the goddess of love The other figures, which are identified by inscriptions in this scene, also have symbolical significance: Nemesis, that is, the

HIMEROS   PARIS   HEIMARMENE

divine vengeance that is turned on those who commit serious crimes, portends that adultery will be severely punished, as she conspicuously points out Helen to the goddess Tyche, who is standing next to her. Also present in the scene is Heimarmene, the destiny that no-one can escape, and finally the winged Himeros, who is in conversation with Paris and whose words fan his illicit desire even further.

It was the will of the gods that Paris should leave Sparta with Helen, for this act of impiety would lead to war between the Achaians and the Trojans and therefore satisfy Gaia's demands.

This myth was embellished by the ancient tragedians, who added that the underlying cause of the war was the terrible curse that lay upon the house of Atreus, the father of Agamemnon and Menelaos. Their misfortunes began with Tantalos, who ruled over a large area of Asia Minor, probably the region of Lydia. Tantalos was very popular with the gods and often dined with them on Mount Olympos; on one occasion, however, he decided to test the wisdom of the immortals and gave a dinner in their honour, at which he offered them his son, Pelops, to eat. The gods at once realised the deceit and were angered at the arrogance of their favourite. They brought the unfortunate Pelops back to life, by sewing the pieces of him together, and condemned his father to eternal torment by hunger and thirst in the midst of a lake with an abundance of water and rich vegetation.

When Pelops reached marriageable age, he learned that Oinomaos, the king of Pisa in Elis, had announced that any youth who succeeded in defeating him in a chariot race would marry his daughter. The king adored his daughter, Hippodameia, however, and therefore never allowed anyone to beat him; he obliged the suitors to take the bride-to-be with them in their chariot during the contest, which acted as a handicap and allowed Oinomaos always to win. Pelops learned of Oinomaos's trick and decided to pay him back in the same coin. By his persuasive words and promises, he won over the king's faithful charioteer, Myrtilos, who loosened the lynch-pin in one of the wheels of Oinomaos's chariot, causing his death. When Myrtilos later asked for his reward, Pelops killed him so that there would be no witness to his deceit; before he died, however, the charioteer cursed him.

Pelops married Hippodameia and became king in the Peloponnese; his kingdom was blessed by the gods, because Hermes gave him the sacred sceptre of authority which had originally been presented to Zeus by Hephaistos. From their marriage were born two sons, Atreus and Thyestes, and a daughter, Nikippe; Pelops also had a third, illegitimate son, Chrysippos, on whom he doted. This relationship aroused the fatal jealousy of his wife, who conspired with her

1

two sons to kill Chrysippos. The curse of Myrtilos had brought disaster to the kingdom of Pelops who, crushed by the death of his beloved son, cursed his own family: to escape their father's wrath, Atreus and Thyestes fled to their sister, who had married king Sthenelos and lived at Mycenae.

The curse of Pelops was to sow discord between the two brothers when, years later, they aspired to the throne of Mycenae. Sthenelos was originally succeeded by his son, Eurystheus, but when he was killed by the descendants of Herakles, the throne had to be occupied by one of the Pelopidai. Although Atreus, as first-born son, had inherited the sacred sceptre of authority from his father, Thyestes managed to cheat his brother and rule himself. Zeus could not permit so great an injustice, however, and intervened to restore order. When Atreus became king, he learned that his brother had attempted to cheat him, and indeed to attain his end had an affair with his wife, Aerope. Blinded with rage, Atreus killed Thyestes' children after which he invited Thyestes to the palace on the pretext of a reconciliation and served him his own children for dinner. When Thyestes became aware of this terrible crime, he cursed his brother and his descendants and left Mycenae; in his despair he turned to the oracle to ask how

2

he could be avenged, and he was told that the son he would bear by his own daughter would destroy the family of Atreus.

And indeed, the incestuous relationship between Thyestes and his daughter Pelopia produced Aigisthos, who was abandoned by his mother in the mountains, out of shame at her impious act. There he was found by Atreus who, unaware of his identity,

1. After the end of the chariot race, Pelops has taken Hippodameia in his chariot and leaves Elis. In the background are depicted two courting doves, a symbolical reference to the future marriage of the young couple. (Amphora, c. 420-410 BC. Arezzo, Archaeological Museum 1460.)

2. Zeus, transformed into a swan, couples with Leda, the wife of Tyndareus. (Statue of Roman date. Rome, Museo Capitolino.)

MYRTILOS   STEROPE   OINOMAOS   ZEUS

took him in and brought him up as his own child. Eventually Thyestes reappeared at Mycenae, and the king sent Aigisthos to kill him, but his father recognised him as his son and conspired with him to kill Atreus. With the aid of Aigisthos, who had been born to destroy the Atreidai, Thyestes succeeded in seizing the sceptre of power from his brother and ascending to the throne of Mycenae, while Atreus's children, Agamemnon and Menelaos, fled to Sparta.

The kingdom of Sparta was ruled by Tyndareus with his wife Leda and their children the Dioskouroi (Kastor and Polydeukes), Helen and Klytaimnestra. Tradition has it that the Dioskouroi and Helen were the children of Zeus, who had approached the enchanting Leda in the form of a swan; this accounts for the courage of the two heroes and the incomparable beauty of their sister. Tyn-

PELOPS   HIPPODAMEIA

The preparations for the chariot race between Pelops and Oinomaos. (East pediment of the temple of Zeus at Olympia, c. 470-456 BC. Olympia, Archaeological Museum.)

dareus affectionately welcomed the children of Atreus to his palace and treated them like a father. When they grew up he married Agamemnon to Klytaimnestra and helped him to return to Mycenae to claim the throne of his father, while to Menelaos he gave his beautiful daughter Helen, and appointed him his successor to the throne of Sparta.

The brothers were rulers of the most important kingdoms in the Peloponnese, at Mycenae and Sparta. Agamemnon and Klytaimnestra had three children, Iphigeneia, Orestes and Elektra, while Menelaos and Helen had an only daughter, Hermione. Their happiness could not last long, however, since it was overshadowed by the heavy curses of their ancestors – Myrtilos, Pelops and Thyestes. And when the goddess Aphrodite sent Paris to Sparta, their lives took a dramatic turn.

115

THE PREPARATIONS FOR THE EXPEDITION

As we have just seen, the 'fair Helen' went with her young suitor to Troy, either through force or through persuasion. The abduction of his wife was a great insult to Menelaos, who immediately began preparations for war in order to defend the honour of his family. In this he was greatly assisted by the oath given by the suitors of Helen to her father, Tyndareus. Helen's beauty was famous throughout the whole of Greece, and when she reached marriageable age, there were many who aspired to her hand. Tyndareus wanted to be sure that the other suitors would accept his decision without protest, and made them swear an oath that they would all jointly defend the honour of his daughter if anyone should ever insult her. Since the strongest kings of Greece were bound by this oath, Menelaos quickly assembled the army he needed.

The wise king of Pylos, Nestor, predicted that if the expedition were to be successful it was essential to secure the participation of Achilles, even though he was not one of Helen's suitors. Achilles was the son of Peleus and Thetis; the divine Nereid knew, however, that if her son took part in the war, he would risk being killed. Although she had attempted to make her child immortal by placing his body on the fire immediately after his birth, the heel by which she had held him remained vulnerable. To protect her cherished son, the goddess had hidden him in the palace of Lykomedes on Skyros, where the hero grew up with the daughters of the king. Odysseus sought him out there and made him reveal his identity through a ruse. Achilles agreed to go with Odysseus, leaving behind him his son Neoptolemos, who had been born to him by one of the daughters of Lykomedes. Achilles was accompanied by his army, the powerful Myrmidons; these were ants that had been turned into human beings by Zeus for his son, Aiakos, the king of Aegina and father of Peleus.

The Greek forces finally gathered at Aulis, from where they were to embark on their long voyage. It was then, however, that the first piece of ill-fortune occurred: as Agamemnon was hunting in the sacred forest of Artemis he killed one of her deer. The goddess was incensed at the hero's presumption, and caused the winds to drop, so that it would be impossible for the ships to put to sea. The prophet Kalchas, who was accompanying the army, predicted that the only way to propitiate the goddess would be to sacrifice the first-born daughter of the king, Iphigeneia. Again it was Odysseus who undertook to go to Mycenae. By telling Klytaimnestra that Iphigeneia was to become the wife of Achilles, he managed to bring her away with him. Meanwhile, in Aulis, the preparations had been made for the sacrifice; when Agamemnon raised his sword to kill his child, however, Artemis felt sorry for the girl and took her away from the altar, replacing her with a deer; the goddess took Iphigeneia to Tauris (on the Crimean peninsula) where she became a priestess in her sanctuary there.

When the Greeks had sacrificed the deer, believing it to be Agamemnon's daughter, favourable winds began to blow and the ships set off on their voyage; one of their ports of call was Delos, where they paid honour to Apollo. Finally, after various adventures, the Greeks arrived at the port of Troy and encamped outside the walls of the city.

Agamemnon raises his knife to sacrifice Iphigeneia, while Artemis replaces the girl with a deer. (South Italian krater, c. 370-350 BC. British Museum F 159.)

THE TENTH YEAR OF THE SIEGE AND THE END OF THE EXPEDITION

1. The spring at which Achilles set an ambush to capture Troilos, because, according to an oracle, if the young son of Priam lived beyond his twentieth year the city of Troy would never fall into enemy hands. (Volute Krater, c. 570 BC. Florence 4209.)

For nine long years the Greek army had been besieging Troy and the city had not fallen. The events of the war had thrown the entire Greek world into turmoil, and indeed the gods themselves, who closely followed the outcome of the struggle from Mount Olympos, were divided into two camps: Hera, Athena, Poseidon, Hermes, and Hephaistos supported the Greeks, while Ares, Apollo, Artemis, Leto and Aphrodite were on the side of the Trojans (see p. 159).

Many heroes distinguished themselves for their courage in the clashes that took place over this time. Outstanding amongst them was Achilles, who captured Troilos (one of Priam's sons) at a spring outside the wall of Troy and then sacrificed him to Apollo. He also excelled in all the battles, leading his army courageously both in attacks on the walls of Troy and in raids on neighbouring areas to gain supplies. Achilles had won some valuable booty from these raids, including two beautiful girls

2

Breseis and Chryseis. Breseis was the daughter of Breseus and lived with her husband Mynetos at Lyrnessos, from where Achilles abducted her to make her his mistress; Chryseis, who was priestess of Apollo on the island of Chryse, was in Thebes in Asia Minor (on the coast of Adramyttion) when Achilles invaded the city and, entranced by her beauty, abducted her to give her to Agamemnon.

The myth took a dramatic turn when Chryses, the father of Chryseis, who was also in service in the sanctuary of Apollo, came to Troy intending to offer ransom to purchase the freedom of his daughter. Agamemnon at first refused to be parted from his beautiful mistress, not realising that his decision would incur the anger of Apollo. And indeed the god punished his impiety by spreading a pestilence and great destruction in the Greek camp.

2. Achilles and Ajax play chess during a lull in the battle. (Amphora, 530 BC. Vatican, Museo Gregoriano 16757.)

Agamemnon was then obliged to give way, but on condition that Achilles would give him Breseis. A delegation was immediately appointed to bring the girl from Achilles' tent to the tent of the king of Mycenae. The Greek leaders had to find a compromise solution to temper the wrath of the gods as quickly as possible, otherwise their army was in danger of being wiped out. This decision, however, slighted Achilles, who in protest withdrew from the battle, together with his warriors.

Although the rest of the forces continued their attacks for some time without Achilles' assistance, the Trojans came very close to the Greek camp at one stage and threatened to capture it. Alarmed, Patroklos, asked his close friend, Achilles, to lend him his army so that he could enter the battle and save the situation. Recognising the seriousness of the turn of events, Achilles agreed on condition that Patroklos would merely hold off the Trojans and would not go on to the attack; he then gave his friend his powerful weapons and ordered the Myrmidons to fight at his side.

When Patroklos entered the battle wearing Achilles' armour, everyone believed that it was the hero himself, who had decided to swallow his wrath in view of the critical situation. The Trojans were thrown into panic at the sight of the fearsome warrior and turned to flight. In his enthusiasm at his success, Patroklos ignored the terms of the agreement he had made with his friend, and started an attack to capture the city. Apollo, however, was watching the battle from the walls of Troy, supporting the inhabitants of city, and checked Patroklos's impetus by wounding him with one of his

1-2. (Kylix, c. 480 BC. British Museum E 76.)

1. Breseis is led to Agamemnon's tent despite the protests of Achilles, who has withdrawn to his own tent.

2. Breseis returns to Achilles after the death of Patroklos.

1

arrows. By the time the hero had realised what had happened and had regrouped his men, Hektor had fatally wounded him. A fierce battle followed to prevent the body of Patroklos falling into the hands of the enemy and the Greeks finally managed, with great difficulty, to bring the dead man back to their camp.

Achilles' grief at the loss of his beloved fellow warrior and friend was unbearable. His comrades tried in vain to alleviate his suffering and Agamemnon immediately returned Breseis to him without demanding any recompense. The hero could think of nothing but revenge, however, and, overwhelmed by his sorrow, asked his mother to procure some new armour for him. Thetis knew that if her son

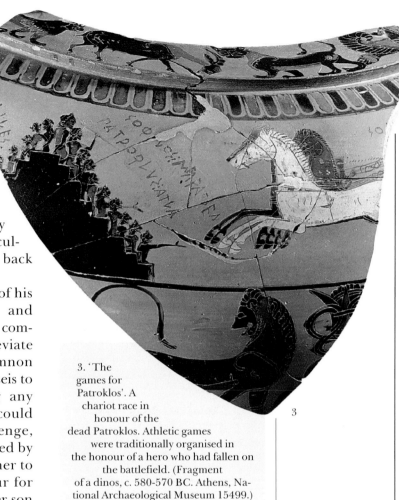

3. 'The games for Patroklos'. A chariot race in honour of the dead Patroklos. Athletic games were traditionally organised in the honour of a hero who had fallen on the battlefield. (Fragment of a dinos, c. 580-570 BC. Athens, National Archaeological Museum 15499.)

2

entered battle again he would be killed, but Achilles was obdurate and ignored her warnings. the Nereid had no other choice but to help him, and went to Hephaistos's workshop and asked him to make new weapons within a single day (see p. 203). Homer gives a detailed description of the elaborate shield of Achilles, which the god of metallurgy adorned with a vast number of representational scenes. Thetis was moved by this and took the weapons to Achilles, who at once assembled his army and rushed into battle to exact his revenge on the man who had caused him such great grief. Hektor soon realised that he would not return alive from this clash, but his conscience and character would not allow him to submit. He bravely fought a duel with Achilles and died a hero's death. The victor, blinded by the pain and anger that

2

were tormenting his soul, tied the body of the dead Hektor to his chariot and dragged it all over the battlefield. When the light of day fell and the bloodshed stopped, Priam, the king of Troy and Hektor's father, came to Achilles' tent and offered a

1. The duel between Achilles and Hektor. (Volute krater, c. 490 BC. British Museum E 468.)

1

3   4

2-4. Achilles drags the body of Hektor behind his chariot. (Lekythos, c. 510 BC. Delos Museum 546.)

ransom for the body of his son, so that he could bury it in his own land. The sight of the crushed father overcame Achilles' refusal, and he complied with his request.

Over the following days Achilles continued to fight with the same strength. His most famous contest was with Memnon, the king of the Ethiopians and ally of the Trojans. Memnon was also the son of a goddess; he had been born by Eos, who brought the dawn, and his father was Tithonos, Priam's brother. Despite this, Achilles managed to defeat him and immediately began an attack on the walls of Troy. Apollo, however, ever vigilant for the safety of the city, directed Paris's arrows to the vulnerable heel of Achilles, causing the death of the hero. Telamon-ian Ajax, from Salamis, at once lifted Achilles' body on to his shoulders, while the other Greeks fought around him, opening a path for him to return to the camp.

The death of Achilles caused great grief amongst the Achaians, who organised in his honour the athletic competitions that were usually held in the memory of heroes, and then buried him together with his beloved friend Patroklos. The elaborate weapons of Achilles, to which both Odysseus and Telamonian Ajax laid claim, were given to Odysseus after a vote; the decision was influenced by the goddess Athena, who knew that the wily king of Ithake would make a major contribution to the success of the expedition. Ajax felt himself slighted

123

because his great strength had been disparaged, and put an end to his own life.

Despite these unpleasant events, the Greek leaders summoned an assembly with the aim of arriving at a strategic design to capture Troy. Their decisions were significantly influenced by the prophetic words spoken by the seer Kalchas, who predicted that if their aim was to be achieved, the following had to happen: Achilles' son, Neoptolemos, had to be summoned to the battle; the weapons of Herakles had to be used, which were in the possession of Philoktetetes (see p. 82), whom they had abandoned injured on the island of Lemnos before they even reached Troy; and the Palladion had to be stolen. The Palladion was the sacred wooden statue of Athena which was said to have fallen from heaven (*diipetes*) and to have been found by Troas, the founder of Troy and his father

1. Ajax lifts the body of the dead Achilles on to his shoulders to take it from the battlefield. (Volute krater, c. 570 BC Florence 4209.)

2. Memnon, with the support of a Trojan, fights a duel with Achilles. (Detail from the east frieze of the Treasury of the Siphnians at Delphi, c. 530 BC. Delphi Museum.)

Laomedon. Troas had set it up in his city and paid it great honour, believing that it was a heaven-sent sign of his power; consequently, if anyone was to steal the Palladion, Troy would lose the symbol of its strength and would be destroyed.

These were the prophecies made by Kalchas and Odysseus set out to carry them out. First he went to Skyros to meet Neoptolemos, who followed him readily. Next he found Philoktetes on Lemnos, but he was bitter and disenchanted with his comrades, because they had abandoned him, and refused to help now that they needed him. Odysseus managed to get Herakles' weapons from Philoktetes by a cunning ruse, however, and

3. Ajax commits suicide. (Metope from the Treasury of the Heraion at Paestum, c. 570-560 BC. Paestum Museum.)

3

the latter had no other choice but to follow him. When they got back to Troy, the camp doctors healed the hero's wound, and he rushed into battle and killed Paris with his deadly arrows. Menelaos's rival was now dead and the war had taken a turn in favour of the Greeks.

The stealing of the Palladion from the city of Troy was the most difficult of all Odysseus's tasks, and once again he had to call upon all his cunning and guile. First he dressed as a beggar and spent the night within the walls of the city. He was recognised by no-one except the 'fair Helen', who had now lost her lover-husband and had been obliged to marry another of Priam's sons, Deiphobos, against her will, so that she had begun to feel homesick. Helen readily agreed to show Odysseus the place where the sacred statue of Pallas Athena was kept. That evening the hero returned to the Greek camp and selected Diomedes to help him, and the two heroes prepared for their dangerous mission. They again spent the night within the walls of the city, made their way to the goddess's sanc-

1. Diomedes carries the Palladion to the Greek camp from the temple of Athena in Troy. (Kylix, c. 400-390 BC. Oxford 1931.39.)

1

2. The Greek soldiers inside the Wooden Horse. (Amphora with relief decoration, c. 670 BC. Mykonos Museum 2240.)

tuary, killing the guards that they met on their way, and succeeded in taking the Palladion without being seen. As they returned, Diomedes led the way carrying the statue, and Odysseus guarded the rear with his sword.

Athena implanted another design in Odysseus's mind, which supplemented his successful capture of the Palladion; this, of course, was the device of the Wooden Horse. The hero got the camp carpenter to make a huge wooden horse, big enough to hold a military unit in its hollow belly. In this way, the Greeks would enter Troy and capture it. But how were they to persuade the Trojans to take the Wooden Horse into their city? Odysseus's plan was indeed very wily: he first chose the warriors who would accompany him in the belly of the horse, and then the rest of the Greeks struck camp, embarked on their ships and, led by Agamemnon, sailed out of the harbour of Troy and anchored off the island of Tenedos. Those left behind took the Wooden Horse to the walls of Troy, leaving in the camp only Sinon, who was to put the plan into practice.

Sinon pretended that he was being hunted, and hid in some vegetation, intending the enemy to see him. The Trojans, who were bewildered by the sight of the Wooden Horse, at once captured him intending to get as much information as they could out of him. Sinon was not loth to talk, and began by saying that his fellow countrymen had left, going on to reveal to them the whole story: Athena had been angered by the theft of the Palladion and had sent great disasters to punish the Greeks; in the confusion, Kalchas had prophesied that the only way to propitiate the goddess was to take the Palladion to Greece and to offer the Wooden Horse in her temple in Troy. Sinon went on to explain his own position: he said that because of his differences with Odysseus, he had become alienated from his fellow warriors. When the ships were preparing to depart, Kalchas announced that they had to sacrifice Sinon to secure the favour of the gods and a favourable wind, as they had done at Aulis with Iphigeneia. In the end, he had managed to escape from the altar and had thus remained behind at Troy.

Sinon's story was believed by the Trojans, who brought the Wooden Horse inside their city and began to celebrate the end of the war. The only ones to realise the misfortune, were Laokoon and Aeneas. Laokoon attempted to warn his fellow countrymen, but was not believed; while he was sacrificing to Poseidon, two serpents emerged from the sea and strangled him together with one of his sons, and the Trojans interpret-

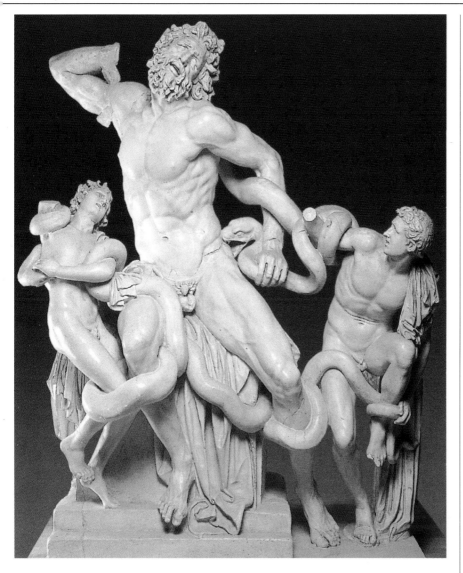

Laokoon and
his son struggle to
escape Poseidon's
serpents.
(Marble statue,
1st c. AD.
Vatican
Museums.)

ed his death as divine punishment because he had not believed in the sanctity of the Wooden Horse. Aeneas was a son of Aphrodite and Anchises (a nephew of Laomedon); since he was the son of a goddess, he knew that this event was a bad omen, and he therefore took care to protect his family by re-moving it from Troy, so that the race of the Trojans, which would soon be destroyed, would not be lost forever.

The capture of Troy was well planned. When the Trojans were completely disorganised as a result of their celebrations and the wine they had drunk, Sinon ascended to a high point of the city and sent a fire signal to Agamemnon instructing him to return with the ships. Then Odysseus's men emerged from the Wooden Horse, opened the gates of the city, and began a merciless slaughter. The tragic nature of the battle is well caught in a kylix in the Louvre Museum, on which Neoptolemos, the son of Achilles, kills Priam, despite the fact that the latter has taken refuge as a suppliant at the altar of Zeus, and hurls Hektor's son, the young Astyanax, from the walls of the city so as to eliminate the last descendant of the royal family. All around them warriors fight hand-to-hand. An equally horrifying act of sacrilege was perpetrated by Lokrian Ajax from Central Greece, who raped Priam's daughter, Kassandra, even though she had sought protection as a suppliant at the statue of Athena. Athena was shocked at his sacrilegious act, and punished the impious hero by sinking him and his ship as he was returning to his home.

Amidst the panic and bloodshed, Odysseus led Menelaos to his wife. When the betrayed

1

husband saw the cause of all these misfortunes, he raised his sword to kill her but was stopped by her beauty and took her in his arms. Aithra was saved along with Helen; she was the mother of Theseus who had faithfully served her queen all these years, and she was now taken to the boat by her grandsons Akamas and Demophon.

After a ten-year siege, Troy had finally fallen and Menelaos's honour had been restored. The Greeks assembled at their ships, taking much booty with them, including the Trojan women, and prepared to set off back to their homelands. However, they were punished severely for the barbarous and impious acts that they had committed when they entered the city of Troy. The Achaians lost their ships as a result of natural disasters and storms caused by the gods, and many of them met with tragic deaths. Even those who did finally manage to return, had to wander for many years before they did so, and even in their homelands great misfortunes awaited them.

1-2. The fall of Troy. (Kylix, c. 490 BC Louvre G 152.)

2

131

THE END OF THE ATREIDAI

Agamemnon, delighted with his triumph, took his army and fleet and set off back to his own land. The most precious piece of booty he had won was Kassandra; she was the daughter of Priam, to whom Apollo had given the power of prophecy; when she refused to sleep with him, however, the god cursed her that her predictions would never be believed. Kassandra knew well the tragic end that was waiting both for her and for Agamemnon at Mycenae, but since no-one would believe her prophetic words, she silently followed her fate.

During the ten years of war, there had been tragic developments in the palace of Agamemnon, for the triple curse that weighed upon the family had not yet been accomplished. Aigisthos, the son of Thyestes, who had been born to take vengeance on the Atreidai for the sacrilegious act of their father, had succeeded in winning Klytaimnestra to his side. When she heard of the death of Iphigeneia, Klytaimnestra conceived a hatred for her husband and in her despair she sought consolation in the arms of Aigisthos; she sent her son, Orestes, to be brought up in the palace of Strophios, the king of Phokis, and kept only Elektra with her.

This was the situation in Agamemnon's palace, when the king arrived unsuspecting at Mycenae. The presence of Kassandra was one more reason for Klytaimnestra to take revenge

1. Orestes murders Aigisthos in the presence of Elektra and Klytaimnestra. (Drawing from a stamnos, c. 470 BC. Berlin, Staatliche Museen F 2184.)

on her husband. At first she welcomed him with great honours; she had prepared a luxurious bath supposedly for him to relax, but as soon as Agamemnon was unarmed and vulnerable, Aigisthos appeared and killed him. Kassandra shared the same fate.

Aigisthos succeeded Agamemnon and ruled with Klytaimnestra at Argos and Mycenae for eight years. When Orestes grew up, he consulted the oracle of Apollo and decided to return to native country to avenge the death of his father. Orestes came to Mycenae accompanied by his faithful friend, Pylades, the son of the king of Phokis, with whom he had grown up. He first met his sister, Elektra, who told him all that had happened and encouraged him to kill the adulterers. On a stamnos in Berlin the hero, with the support of Elektra, pierces Aigisthos's breast with his sword, while Klytaimnestra threaters him with an axe; she will soon share the fate of her second husband, however.

Despite his motives and intentions, Orestes was nevertheless a matricide, and the Furies could not overlook such an impious crime. The terrible goddesses of the conscience began to pursue the hero relentlessly. Orestes, sought refuge at the Delphic oracle in the hope that Apollo would help him. This episode is depicted a column krater in the Louvre Museum, where a

2

winged Fury pursues Orestes, while he takes refuge at Apollo's altar; the god holds a laurel branch in his hand and turns his gaze on the Fury and restrains her impetus with a gentle gesture of his hand. Orestes was in the end acquitted by the court of the Areopagos in Athens, and the deities of the conscience ceased to persecute him.

In another version of the myth, Orestes meets his lost sister, Iphigeneia. According to an oracle, Orestes would only be completely purified and free of the persecution of the Furies, if he brought the cult statue (xoanon) of Artemis from Tauris to Greece. In the sanctuary of Artemis in Tauris, however, where Iphigeneia was priestess, strangers were sacrificed at the goddess's altar in her honour, and this was the fate awaiting Orestes when he arrived at the sanctuary together with his comrade, Pylades. The two heroes, however, chanced to meet with Iphigeneia, who spoke to them

2. Orestes, pursued by the Furies, takes refuge in the sanctuary of Apollo at Delphi. (Drawing from a column krater, c. 440-430 BC. Louvre K 343.)

1. Orestes has taken refuge at Delphi to escape the Furies. One of the Furies can be seen behind the Delphic tripod threatening him and holding snakes in her hands. The hero turns in despair to Athena, who seems ready to help him, while Apollo avoids his eye and looks at one of the Furies. (South Italian bell krater, c. 350-340 BC. British Museum.)

full of nostalgia for her family and asked them what had been happening in her absence. Their discussion led to the recognition of the brother and sister and, together with Pylades, they took the sacred xoanon of Artemis and returned to their homeland.

Orestes ultimately succeeded to the throne of his father at Mycenae, and moreover added Sparta to his kingdom by taking the daughter of Menelaos as his wife; by his marriage to Hermione he had a son, Teisamenos, who later succeeded him.

During the reign of Te-isamenos, the descendants of Herakles returned to Mycenae. As we have already seen, the Delphic oracle had predicted that the third generation of Her-akleidai would rule in the hero's place of origin, and the interval of time envisaged had now elapsed.

The Herakleidai dethroned Teisamenos and made themselves kings of the most important cities of the Peloponnese. The cycle of the family of Pelops had been come to an end, as, too, had the period when the kingdom of Mycenae was at its height.

EPILOGUE

The events that disturbed the troubled heroic period are preserved in many myths that were handed down in different versions, and which cannot be encapsulated in a brief, concise account.

The basic core of the Trojan myth is formed on the basis of the Epic Cycle, a series of epic poems with a cyclical narrative, which opens with the causes of the war and ends with the return of the heroes to their homeland; the events leading to the Trojan War were recounted in the *Kypria Epe*; Homer's *Iliad* described the tenth year of the siege of Troy and the wrath of Achilles; the *Aithiopis* is an account of Achilles' duel with Memnon, who was king of the Ethiopians and ally of the Trojans; the tragic fall of Troy is narrated in the *Iliou Persis;* the *Nostoi* is an account of the adventures of the Greeks as they return to their homeland; and Homer's *Odyssey* narrates the ten years' wandering of the wily Odysseus before his return to Ithake. The Epic Cycle contains several references to the troubled history of the family of Pelops, Atreus and Agamemnon, but more information on this subject can be derived from the ancient tragedies. The tragedians retained the basic core of the myth as formulated in epic poetry, but embellished it with dramatic elements more appropriate to the spirit of ancient tragedy, thus creating a wide range of different

2. Orestes attacks Klytaimnestra, who raises her arms in an attempt to resist. (Seal, early 4th c. BC. Ioannina Archaeological Museum.)

2

tragedies entitled *Elektra*, and Euripides also deals with Orestes' adventures in his tragedy named after him. Euripides was also inspired by the myth of Iphigeneia and composed his tragedy *Iphigeneia in Aulis* which deals with the sacrifice of the girl to Artemis, and another entitled *Iphigeneia in Tauris*, which describes Orestes' journey to Tauris and his meeting with his lost sister.

As we can see, the myth relating to the rule of Pelops and his descendants in the Peloponnese was very popular in ancient poetry; this circumstance is probably due to its direct connection with the so-called Mycenaean civilisation, which was centred on the kingdom of Mycenae. The outstanding finds brought to light by the excavations of Heinrich Schliemann have shown that between the 14th and 11th century BC there was an important civilisation at Mycenae that enjoyed great prestige and influence; the decline of this civilisation in the 11th century BC is connected with the destruction of the palace at Mycenae.

Many theories have been advanced as to the causes of this destruction, most of them connecting it with the presence of the Dorians in this area. According to one view, the Dorians moved south from Boeotia or Thessaly

versions. The three plays of Aeschylus's trilogy, the *Oresteia*, which was highly popular, were based on a single theme: the events that took place at Mycenae after Agamemnon's return from Troy. The first tragedy is called *Agamemnon*, and describes the king's arrival at Mycenae and his tragic death, the second is called *Choephoroi* and deals with Orestes' matricide and its fearful consequences for the hero, while in the third, the *Eumenides*, Orestes is freed from the persecution of the Furies. The meeting between Orestes and his sister at Mycenae is described by Sophocles and Euripides in two and invaded the Peloponnese at the beginning of the so-called Dark Age (11th c. BC). Other scholars, however, do not believe that the descent of the Dorians was a sudden catastrophic invasion, and assert that they gradually penetrated the Peloponnese and were peacefully assimilated into the local population; according to this latter theory, the Dorians came to power by exploiting the decline of the Mycenaean palaces, which was the result either of economic collapse or destructive natural events such as earthquakes.

According to the myth, the Atreidai were expelled from the Peloponnese when the Herakleidai invaded. After the death of his father Herakles, Hyllos attempted to wrest the throne of Mycenae from Eurystheus; despite killing his opponent, however, he did not succeed in winning power because the oracle at Delphi had predicted that it would only be the third generation of Herakles' descendants who would successfully invade the Peloponnese. In the meantime, power was assumed by the Atreidai, in the following sequence: Atreus, Thyestes, Agamemnon, Aigisthos, Orestes and Teisamenos, who ruled over Mycenae, Argos and Tiryns, the two last also adding Sparta. The downfall of these rulers was their personal passion and thirst for power, and the Trojan war was added to their internecine conflicts with tragic consequences. When the third generation of the Herakleidai returned to the Peloponnese, it had no difficulty in driving from power the last of the family of Atreus: it was in any case the will of the gods.

It is difficult not to associate the mythical invasion of the Herakleidai with the collapse of the powerful kingdom of Mycenae, which is confirmed by archaeological evidence. Unfortunately, however, we can only guess at the causes of this destruction. We do not know what historical events inspired the epic poets to recount the heroic expedition against Troy; the powerful kingdoms of Mycenaean times probably organised military expeditions to distant lands in order to increase their power both territorially and economically. All that we can be certain of is that in the 11th century BC the palace at Mycenae was destroyed and Mycenaean civilisation went into decline; it may be that the Trojan War, or other similar ambitious enterprises, did not yield the expected benefits, and together with a variety of internal conflicts led to the economic collapse of the palace at Mycenaean; or perhaps the gods had concluded that the descendants of the hero Herakles had wandered long enough and the time had come for them to return to their homeland.

Gold funeral mask, the so-called 'mask of Agamemnon'. (From a tomd in Grave Circle A at Mycenae. Middle of the 16th c. BC. Athens, National Archaeological Museum 624.)

ZEUS

POSEIDON

ATHENA

ARTEMIS

ARES

DEMETER

IN GREEK MYTHOLOGY

HERA

HERMES

APOLLO

HEPHAISTOS

APHRODITE

DIONYSOS

THE TWELVE OLYMPIAN GODS
ATHENA

Athena was the daughter of Zeus and the Okeanid Metis, but was born from the head of her omnipotent father. According to the tradition accounting for this myth, when Zeus slept with Metis, he was told that he would have a daughter and a son, and that when the latter grew up he would become more powerful and more intelligent than Zeus himself. The father of the gods decided to swallow his mistress to prevent her giving birth to the male child, who was to threaten his authority and give rise to conflict similar to that of the past. He kept his daughter inside his body, however, and gave birth to her himself. This was a very popular subject in Attic art; on an amphora in the British Museum, the young

1. The birth of Athena from the head of Zeus. (Amphora, c. 520-510 BC. British Museum B 244.)

2. Athena with helmet and spear in an attitude of reflection before a stele, which probably recorded the names of dead Athenians. (Marble relief, c. 470 BC. Athens, Acropolis Museum 695.)

2

1. Athena Promachos. The god wears a helmet and aegis and holds a spear. (Bronze statuette, c. 500-490 BC. Athens, National Archaeological Museum 6447.)

2. Athena Promachos. (Panathenaic amphora, 363/2 BC. Athens, National Archaeological Museum.)

Athena emerges fully armed from the head of Zeus, who is seated and holds his sceptre; next to the father stands Eileithyia, the goddess of childbirth, who is in fact depicted twice on either side of him, while Hermes and Hephaistos are portrayed at the sides of the scene.

The daughter born from the head of the father of the gods inherited from him the gift of wisdom; she was endowed with discretion, intelligence and resourcefulness and devoted herself to both peace and war. She was adroit and had a restless spirit, and was accordingly honoured as the patron of the crafts, with the epithet (Athena) Ergane. Indeed she worked alongside Hephaistos, the god of metallurgy, and it is said that it was from their joint workshop that Prometheus stole the fire that he gave to human beings.

Athena also inherited from her father his strength and courage, and was honoured as the god of war, with the epithet (Athena) Promachos. She distinguished herself for her great courage in the Battle of the Giants, but was not a lover of war, like her brother Ares; she had a strategic rather than an aggressive spirit and did not like bloody conflict. She supported many heroes (such as Herakles, Perseus, Theseus and Jason), helping them to carry out their impossible labours, but she never forgave injustice. During the Trojan War she took the side of the Achaians, and indeed inspired Odysseus to conceive the device of the Wooden Horse, but she severely punished her favourites for the acts of sacrilege they committed when they finally captured Troy. The goddess of

2

1

3. Pallas Athena.
(Drawing by Gyzis
for the flag of the
University of
Athens, 1887.
Bank of Greece
Collection.)

3

1. Athena Promachos. (Panathenaic amphora, 566 BC. British Museum.)

2. Athena with helmet, aegis, spear and shield, on which is depicted a gorgoneion. (Drawing from an amphora, c. 490 BC. Basel Ka 418.)

wisdom, war and the arts was indomitable and completely self-sufficient, and therefore rejected ties of marriage; the epithets (Athena) Parthenos and (Athena) Pallas (which means girl) stressed her purity.

In art Athena is normally depicted fully armed, carrying a shield and holding a spear. Her most characteristic symbol and also her most powerful weapon is the aegis that she wore on her breast; this was the skin of a Giant, who yielded to the goddess's strength during the battle of the Giants. The centre of the aegis is normally dominated by the gorgoneion, the head of the gorgon Medusa, which was given to Athena by her protege, Perseus; the gorgoneion is flanked by fearsome serpents and had the deadly power to petrify with its gaze anyone who dared to look at it.

The gold and ivory statue of Athena is very famous; this was made by Pheidias to adorn the interior of the Parthenon, her brilliant temple on the Athenian Acropolis; a tribute to the goddess who, by offering the olive to the Athenians, won the right to protect the city. In the monumental cult statue Athena was depicted fully armed, holding a Nike on her right hand and a shield in her left; the shield was decorated with scenes from the Battles of the Amazons and the Giants, while the base of the statue bore a relief scene depicting the birth of Pandora.

1

3. Reconstruction of the east facade of the Parthenon on the Athenian Acropolis (447-432 BC. Drawing by the architect B. Loviot, Ecoles des Beaux Arts.)

The Parthenon, the splendid monument that dominates the sacred rock of the Acropolis, was the centre of the cult of Athena in antiquity. The Great Panathenaia, the most brilliant festival in honour of the patron goddess of the city, was held every four years; a ritual procession started from the Kerameikos, crossed the Agora of the city and ended at the Parthenon to honour the goddess. Athletic contests were organised as part of the festivities, the prizes for the victors being amphoras containing very high quality olive oil —the so-called Panathenaic amphoras– in memory of the precious gift bestowed by the goddess on the Athenians.

4. The Varvakeion Athena. Roman copy (2nd. c. AD) of the gold and ivory cult statue of Athena Parthenos that stood inside the Parthenon. (Athens, National Archaeological Museum 129.)

The Parthenon, the temple of
Athena Parthenos, on the Acropolis. (447-432 BC.)

APOLLO

Apollo was the son of Zeus and Leto and the brother of Artemis. The affair between Leto (daughter of the Titan Koios and Phoibe) and Zeus, enraged Hera, who took revenge on her rival by letting it be known that any place that received her so that she could give birth would be cursed. As a result of Hera's threat, Leto was obliged to wander to many places. After several months, she came to Delos, an island so poor and so arid that no threat could possibly make things worse; Leto persuaded the nymph Delos to take her in, by promising that the son that she would bear would make her island famous

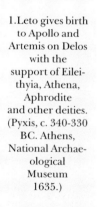

1. Leto gives birth to Apollo and Artemis on Delos with the support of Eileithyia, Athena, Aphrodite and other deities. (Pyxis, c. 340-330 BC. Athens, National Archaeological Museum 1635.)

2

by founding his first sanctuary there. Her torment was not over, however; Hera distracted Eileithyia, the goddess of childbirth, who was her daughter, and as a result Leto suffered birth pains for nine whole months. It was only when the other goddesses sent Iris to Mount Olympos that Eileithyia learned what was happening and hastened to Delos. With the aid of the goddess of childbirth, Leto grasped a palm tree and gave birth to the handsome Apollo. Ever since the palm tree has been the god's sacred tree, and is associated with his cult on the island.

Apollo was the great teacher and patron of the art of music. The invention of his musical instrument, the lyre, however, is not due to the god himself. Tradition has it that it was made from a tortoise shell by Hermes, when he was a child; but the messenger of the gods was more interested in other toys. One day he escaped from his cradle, stole the flocks of Apollo, and having hidden them well, returned to his mother as though nothing had happened. Apollo, who was equally crafty, soon discovered

2. Apollo with his lyre pours a libation from a bowl. (Kylix, c. 480 BC. Delphi Museum 8410.)

the thief. A quarrel broke out between the two gods which was ended by the intervention of Zeus, and their reconciliation was sealed by gifts: Apollo allowed Hermes to look after his flocks and in return received the lyre, through which he cultivated his musical talent.

Nobody could compete with Apollo playing the lyre or the kithara (a stringed instrument of the same type as the lyre), and those who disputed his talent were harshly punished. One of these was the Satyr Marsyas, who had been taught how to play the flute by Athena and indeed enchanted everyone with his playing; when he claimed, however, that his talent was unsurpassable, Apollo was slighted and challenged him to prove it. With his heavenly gift and genius, the god confirmed his superiority and punished Maryas's impiety with a terrible death. The judges in this music competition were the Muses – the nine daughters of Zeus and Mnemosyne (one of the daughters of Ouranos and Gaia), patrons of music, and inspirers of artists; their names

1

2

1-3. The Muses watch the music competition between Apollo and Marsyas. (Slabs from a statue base, c. 325-300 BC. Athens, National Archaeological Museum 215-217.)

are: Kleio, Euterpe, Thaleia, Melpomene, Terpsichore, Erato, Polymnia, Ourania and Kalliope. Three marble reliefs in the Athens National Archaeological Museum, show the Muses listening to the flute-playing of Maryas who is competing with Apollo the kithara player. This myth stresses and explains Apollo's attribute as patron and teacher of music.

Apollo was also famous for his prophetic qualities. Determined to reveal the intentions of his fa-

ther, Zeus, to mankind, he wandered the length and breadth of Greece, looking for the most suitable place to found his oracle. he finally chose Delphi, where he founded his famous pan-Hellenic sanctuary. The fame of the Delphic oracle travelled beyond the borders of the Greek world and every year thousands of visitors consulted the oracle on all kinds of matters, ranging from personal is-

4. The symbols of Apollo and the nine Muses. (Part of a mosaic floor of a villa at Elis, middle of the 3rd c. AD. Elis, Archaeological Collection.)

4

153

sues to major political decisions. The tripod and the omphalos were the sacred symbols of Apollo and were kept in the inner sanctum of his temple at Delphi. On the Delphic tripod sat the Pythia, the priestess who communicated spiritually with the god and transmitted his prophecies. The omphalos was the sacred stone symbolising the position of Delphi at the centre of the world, for it was here that two eagles released by Zeus met on their way from Mount Olympos to opposite ends of the earth.

The god of music was also skilled in the art of medicine. He taught the secrets of medicine to his son, Asklepios, to whom he gave the gift of relieving people's pain and illness. Apollo was also a highly skilled archer, and often accompanied his sister, Artemis, on her hunting expeditions.

In addition to the palm tree, the lyre, the tripod, the omphalos and the bow, the symbols of Apollo include the laurel branch, which is associated with one of the god's amorous adventures. Daphne was a nymph, the daughter of the river god Phineus; Apollo was enchanted by her beauty and attempted despairingly to win her. The girl, however, did not want to submit to the amorous invitation of the god and in her despair sought the aid of her father, who, to rescue her, transformed her into the laurel tree (*daphne*) that took her name. When Apollo saw that he had lost his beloved forever, he established the laurel as the sacred plant of his cult, and wreaths made from its branches were offered as prizes for the victors in the musical competitions held in his honour. The cult of the god Pan is also associated with music and the sacred site at Delphi. Pan was a pastoral god who lived in the mountains and forests; he is described as having the legs of a goat and horns on his head, features that are very reminiscent of the Satyrs who were the followers of Dionysos. He is considered to be the inventor of a type of flute which is known as the 'Pan-pipe' and was famous for the magical quality of his music. In the foothills of Mount Parnassos, near the sanctuary of Apollo, has been found a sacred cave called the Korykeion cave, which was dedicated to Pan and the Nymphs, like many other caves in Greece.

1. Terracotta monument in the shape of a wheel, around the rim of which stand twelve nymphs with Pan playing the pipes in the centre. (From the Korykeion in Cave. Boeotian work, middle of the 5th c. BC. Delphi Museum.)

2. The pastoral god Pan with his pipes. (Marble statuette of Roman times. Elis Archaeological Collection 1338.)

2

The temple of Apollo at Delphi. (4th c. BC.)

ARES

Ares was the son of Zeus and Hera; his sisters were Eileithyia, goddess of childbirth, and Hebe, goddess of youth.

Ares was the god of war, forever thirsting for fierce battles and bloody conflicts. He was sharp-tempered and aggressive by nature, in contrast with his half-sister Athena, who was distin-

1. Aphrodite and Ares. (Kylix, c. 430 BC. British Museum E 82.)

guished by her wisdom and sense of strategy (see pp. 140-147). The events of the Trojan War throw into relief the difference between the two gods of the martial art: Ares watches or takes part in the bloodshed on the side of the Trojans, while Athena assists the Achaians to make and implement the plan which leads them to their final victory (see pp. 128-129).

Despite the fact that Ares was famous for his courage and his handsomeness, he was not very popular with the gods because of his violent, warlike nature.

Nevertheless he managed to enchant Aphrodite, when she was married to Hephaistos (see p. 199), an episode that seriously disturbed the serenity of Mount Olympos. The first to discover the lovers was Helios, as he travelled in his chariot on the stream of Ocean, and he immediately reported it to the deceived husband. The embittered Hephaistos made an invisible net which he placed on his wife's bed in order to catch the couple in the act. The device was indeed effective, and the two lovers soon found themselves trapped in the net, while all the gods laughed at their

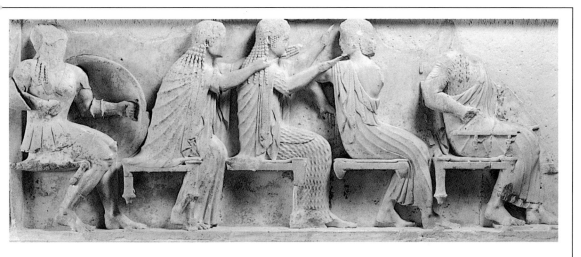

plight. Hephaistos, however, was enraged; only Poseidon was able to calm him, by promising that he would make sure that the adulterer was punished. It was therefore decided that Ares should leave Olympos until the episode was forgotten.

Ares often created problems; he was the first to be judged by

the court of the Areopagos, which was named after him to commemorate this event. This supreme court which only passed judgement on cases of murder, was first constituted when Poseidon accused Ares of violently murdering his son, Halirrhothios. The Areopagos sat in Athens and acquitted the god of war, on the grounds that Halirrhothios had attempted to rape his daughter, Alkippe. The symbols of Ares are associated with arms and armour: the god is usually depicted in full panoply, wearing a helmet, cuirass and greaves, and carrying a shield and spear. His adherents shared his thirst for war and bloodshed. Two of his children, Phobos (Fear) and Deimos (flight) would fight on his side and route his opponents, and he was frequently accompanied by the deity of war Ennyo, acting as his charioteer, and Eris, the goddess of strife.

2. The gods watch the Trojan War: Ares, Aphrodite or Leto, Artemis, Apollo and Zeus. (Part of the east frieze of the Treasury of the Siphnians at Delphi, c. 530 BC.)

3. Ares, the god of war, with his panoply. (Volute krater, c. 570 BC. Florence 4209.)

3

ARTEMIS

A rtemis was the sister of Apollo, and the daughter of Zeus and Leto. She was the goddess of the hunt; she had a gift for taming wild animals and catching all kinds of prey (Mistress of the Animals), and at the same time she was patron goddess of nature and young animals. She spent most of her time living free in the forests, engaging in hunting and archery.

She is frequently accompanied on her hunting expeditions by Apollo, however, who was also an excellent archer. The two children had great love and respect for their mother, and were always eager to defend her hon-our. On one occasion they severely punished Niobe, the sister of Pelops, who lived at Thebes with her husband, and Amphion and their fourteen children, seven sons and seven daughters. Niobe incurred the anger of Apollo and Artemis, because she boasted to her Theban companions that she was a much better mother than Leto. The two gods punished her for her impious words by hunting down and killing her children. The episode is depicted on a kalyx krater in the Louvre Museum: Apollo shoots his arrows at the sons of Niobe, while Artemis attacks her daughters.

1. Ivory head with gold ornaments. (Probably from a cult statue of Artemis, 6th c. BC. Delphi Museum.)

2. Artemis and Apollo shoot their arrows at the children of Niobe. (Kalyx krater, c. 460-450 BC. Louvre G 341.)

The goddess of the hunt denied love, like her half-sister, Athena. She also severely punished anyone who did not respect her wishes. The hunter Aktaion, who dared to lie in hiding in order to see her bathe naked, met with a dramatic end; the goddess quickly realised he was watching her and turned him into a deer, after which she ordered her dogs to turn on him and tear him apart. Artemis

4

4. Artemis with her bow and a deer. (Terracotta figurine, c. 480 BC. Corfu, Archaeological Museum.)

3. Artemis hunts a deer. (Marble sculpture, 150-100 BC. Delos Museum A 449.)

3

1. Apollo with his kithara, Artemis with her bow, and their mother Leto, pour libations around the omphalos at Delphi, accompanied by Hermes. (Volute krater, c. 420-400 BC. British Museum E 502.)

2. Artemis as 'Mistress of the Animals'. (Amphora, 520-500 BC. Basel, Archaeological Museum and Ludwig Collection.)

was also regarded as the patron of young women and childbirth. Despite the fact that she herself denied the bonds of marriage, her worship was associated with the marriage ritual. Every bride-to-be dedicated her toys to the goddess, thus leaving the objects associated with her carefree childhood behind her, and assumed the responsibilities of wife; this symbolical act prepared every girl for marriage, the transition from her father's house to the house of her husband. Married women too, however did not neglect the worship of Artemis, because they believed that she protected them during childbirth, and decided on the fate of pregnant women; to propitiate her, they

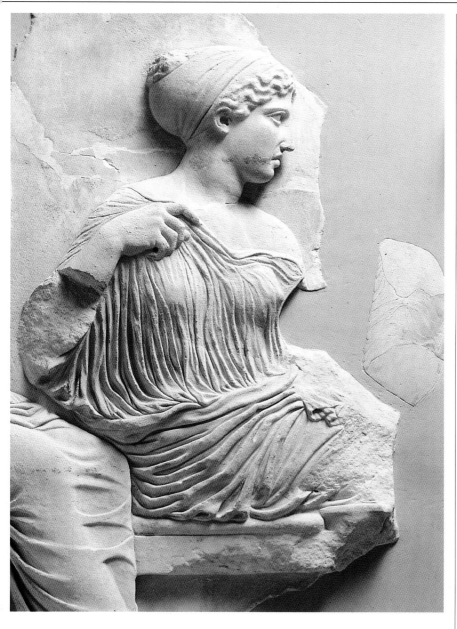

3. Artemis at the assembly of the gods depicted on the east frieze of the Parthenon. (447-432 BC. Athens, Acropolis Museum.)

dedicated the chitons of women who had died during childbirth or during confinement, in the sanctuary of the goddess at Brauron in Attica.

The symbols of Artemis are her hunting weapons: the bow, quiver and arrows, and her sacred animal is the deer. The goddess can by identified by her quiver and bow on a column krater in the British Museum, on which she is accompanied by Apollos, Hermes and Leto.

163

The stoa of the bears in the sanctuary
of Artemis at Brauron.

APHRODITE

When Ouranos was castrated by Kronos, his seed fell into the sea and gave birth to Aphrodite; the goddess emerged from the foaming waves on Cyprus and dazzled the world with her beauty.

Aphrodite was the goddess of love; she planted desire in the souls of mortals and immortals alike and impelled them both to marriage and to adultery. Her wishes were carried out by her faithful acolyte, the winged Eros, who made his victims fall in love with his arrows. When Paris-Alexander had to decide which of the goddesses should be given the apple of Eris, he could resist neither Aphrodite's beauty nor the gift that she offered him; he gave the apple to the most beautiful of the goddesses and won the love of Helen, the fairest of all women, heedless of the consequences of his decision (see pp. 108-110) Aphrodite also sent Eros to

1. Aphrodite bathing. (Marble statuette, c. 100 BC. Rhodes, Archaeological Museum.)

2. Aphrodite accompanied by small figures of winged Eros. (Kylix, c. 490-480 BC. Berlin, Staatliche Museen F 2291.)

2

Medea, in order to help Jason escape from Kolchis (see pp. 226-228).

Aphrodite enchanted everyone with her charm. Many of the gods, and also ordinary mortals, attempted to win her, and she often revealed her own choices: she competed with Persephone for the love of the handsome Adonis, and disappointed the goat-footed Pan (see p. 169). She was compelled, however, to marry Hephaistos against her will. This marriage was the price exacted by Hephaistos for freeing his mother, Hera, from the invisible chains of her throne; the god of metallurgy had made a throne-trap

3

3. Aphrodite seated on a goat. (Scene on the cover of a bronze mirror, c. 370 BC. Louvre 1707.)

4. The Aphrodite of Milos (Venus de Milo). The goddess of love was the first respectable woman that artists dared to depict naked, because of her matchless beauty. (Marble statue, 150-125 BC. Louvre.)

4

1   2   3

1-3. Aphrodite and her followers in an idyllic setting. (Pyxis, c. 420-400 BC. British Museum E 775.)

to avenge himself on his mother who had rejected him because he was a cripple (see pp. 198-199). In spite of all the gods, Hephaistos desired to marry the beautiful Aphrodite, and it was only when his demand was met that he agreed to free his mother. The goddess of love, however, could not reconcile herself to a marriage into which she had been compelled to enter. She quickly humiliated her husband by finding consolation in the arms of Ares (see pp. 158-159).

From this relationship between the goddess of love, who revitalises humans, and the god of war, who spreads death, was born Harmonia; the union of life and death gave perfection to the world.

Aphrodite's retinue included many other minor deities, as well as Eros. Some of these are identified by inscriptions on a pyxis in the British Museum: in an idyllic setting, Aphrodite stands behind her chariot, which is pulled by Pothos and Edylogos: Eunomia

4

and Harmonia are seated and hold wreaths, Daidia and Himeros (who causes erotic desire) each hold a necklace, and Eudaimonia is tying her sandal. The goddess's attendants also included Hebe, the goddess of youth, the Hours, Eunomia, Dike and Eirene, the daughters of Zeus and Themis, and the Graces, Aglaia, Euphrosyne and Thaleia, who were daughters of Zeus and Eurynome.

4. Terracotta figurine of Eros.
(350-300 BC. Pella Museum.)

5. The pastoral god Pan flirts with Aphrodite, and the godess tries to deter him by threatening him with her sandal.
(Marble sculpture, c. 100 BC. Athens, National Archaeological Museum 3335.)

5

DEMETER

1. Head of the cult statue of Demeter from her temple at Dion. (320-300 BC. Dion Museum.)

2. Demeter, holding a sceptre in her left hand, gives Triptolomos the ears of corn, while Persephone, holding the torches, blesses him. (Marble relief, c. 440-430 BC. Athens, National Archaeological Museum 126.)

Demeter was the daughter of Kronos and Rhea; when her brother Zeus deposed his father and seized power, he took her with him to Mount Olympos and assigned to her the task of protecting vegetation and farming. On one occasion he slept with her and gave her a beautiful daughter, Persephone.

The cult of Demeter and Persephone was very important in ancient Greece, and its establishment is accounted for by the following myth. One day Kore was playing happily with her friends in the fields, when she was seen by the god of the Underworld, Pluto, who fell in love with her. He immediately rushed up to earth in his chariot and, with the agreement of Zeus, seized her to carry her off to his gloomy kingdom. As she was leaving the light of day behind her forever, Persephone called on her mother for help. It was too late, however, for Hades' chariot had already plunged into the bowels of the earth. Demeter wandered the whole world in her despair, searching for her child, until Helios took pity on her and told her the truth. In her distress, the goddess continued to wander from place to place until she came to Eleusis. Eleusis was ruled by Keleos, with his wife Metaneira, their four daughters and new-born only son, Demophon. Demeter pretended that she was a simple old woman and persuaded Metaneira to take her on as nurse to her only son. In order to reward the hospitable family, she secretly placed the small Demophon on the fire every night with the intention of making him immortal. One night, however, she was seen by Metaneira, who in her terror

1

began to call out for help. Demeter then revealed her true identity and demanded that the inhabitants of Eleusis build a temple and altar in her honour, so as to atone for their impiety and lack of belief; and so the famous sanctuary at Eleusis was founded. The goddess then shut herself up in her temple and caused a terrible drought on earth, to compel the gods to return her daughter to her. Humans began to die of hunger and thirst, and the need to find some solution became ever more pressing. After Zeus's intervention, Pluto was finally persuaded to be parted from his wife in order to save mankind. Before he lost her for-

ever, however, he put a pomegranate into her mouth, knowing that the taste of this earthly fruit would oblige her to return to him. This ruse obliged the gods to find a compromise; it was decided that for one third of the year Persephone would live with her husband, spending the rest of the year with her mother.

The myth of Persephone is an interpretation of the cycle of the seasons, and a symbol of the alternation between life and death. For the four months of the winter, when Kore lives in the Underworld, nature lies dead and fruit is frozen; but when she ascends from the gloom of Hades to keep her

1. Triptolomos sets off to teach men the benefits of farming. (Skyphos, c. 480 BC. British Museum E 140.)

1

2. Pluto has seized Persephone in his arms and makes off swiftly in his chariot, while Hermes runs in front and clears the way. The girl attempts to escape reaching her arms out in despair, with agony etched on her face. One of her friends looks on in terror and raises her arm to protect herself. (Wall-painting in the 'tomb of Persephone' at Vergina, middle of the 4th c. BC.)

mother company on earth, she brings spring with her, and the whole of nature celebrates her arrival and is reborn, to give its fruits. The ascent of Persephone from Hades – the triumph of life over death – was probably celebrated in the famous Eleusinian Mysteries, the secret rituals that took place in the sanctuary of Demeter at Eleusis. The curators of the sanctuary supervised the gradual initiation of believers into the sacred mysteries of the cult of Demeter, but they bound the initiates by a solemn oath never to reveal the rituals. Consequently the rites that took place at the festival are still unknown today; they probably took the form of a ceremony welcoming Persephone to the Upper world, designed to reconcile man to death and give him spiritual tranquillity.

The goddess who was responsible for the rebirth of nature, and her mother, the patron goddess of cereals, taught the benefits of farming to men; the mission was undertaken by Triptolemos, one of their priests at Eleusis. A skyphos in the British Museum depicts the departure of Triptolemos; the young messenger with the sacred ears of corn in his hand will wander the world on a winged chariot pulled by two serpents; in his right hand he holds the bowl into which Persephone is pouring a libation from an oinochoe, to seal the sanctity of his mission. She is accompanied by the nymph Eleusis, and Demeter stands on the winged chariot, holding the symbols of the Eleusinian cult: the ears of corn and the torch.

The ears of corn are the sacred fruit of the goddess of farming and cereals, and the torch alludes to the rituals of the Eleusinian Mysteries which took place at night by torch-light.

ZEUS

Zeus was the son of Kronos and Rhea; when he grew to manhood he deposed his father and, after hard battles fought against the Titans and Giants, became king of the gods and men. He gathered around him his brothers and sisters and some of his children and created the pantheon of the twelve gods of Olympos. These gods dwelt on the peaks of the mountain and oversaw everything that happened in the world.

The omnipotent god was worshipped in many different forms. The altar to him in the courtyards of houses was normally erected to Zeus Herkeios, who protected the family hearth. Zeus Xenios was the god of hospitality, and all travellers had to be welcomed in

1. Head of a bearded man, probably Zeus. (Dion, Archaeological Museum.)

2. Zeus and Hera hold royal sceptres and sit on banquet couches. (Kylix, c. 440-430 BC. British Museum E 82.)

his honour. Zeus Polieus was guardian of cities, Zeus Horkios oversaw the observance of oaths, and Zeus Soter was a general protector and benefactor. The oracle of Zeus at Dodona was the oldest in the world and enjoyed fame equal to that of Apollo at Delphi. It attracted large numbers of visitors from many different places and was an important cult centre. The god's priestesses made their prophecies by interpreting the cooing of doves and the rustling of the leaves of a sacred oak tree.

There was also an important

3. Head of Zeus. (Bronze coin of Elis, 271-191 BC. Athens, Numismatic Museum.)

4. Head of Zeus. (Silver coin of Elis, 323-271 BC. Athens, Numismatic Museum.)

5. Monumental statue of Zeus, who was probably holding a thunderbolt in his right hand. (c. 460 BC. Athens, National Archaeological Museum 15161.)

3

4

5

1. Bronze statuette of Zeus holding the thunderbolt. (c. 460 BC. Athens, National Archaeological Museum 16546.)

cult of Zeus in the famous sanctuary at Olympia. His temple here was dominated by the monumental gold and ivory statue made by the Athenian sculptor Pheidias (437-430 BC). The altar to the god was formed of the ashes of the sacrifices made in his honour, and his priests divined his prophecies by examining the entrails of the sacrificial victims. The sanctuary at Olympia became famous both for its oracle, and because it was there that Herakles founded the Olympic Games in honour of his heavenly father.

In art Zeus is depicted as a venerable bearded man and holds a sceptre as a symbol of power, while his strength is also symbolised by the thunderbolt and the eagle. The thunderbolt was the mighty weapon made specially for him by the Kyklopes; he used it in his battles against the Titans and Giants and also to impose order and justice in the world. Zeus threw his thunderbolt to resolve the dispute between Apollo and Herakles over the Delphic tripod (see pp. 79-80) and used the same weapon when he took the life of Asklepios, because he believed that he was a threat to his own omnipotence. A bronze statue in the Athens National Archaeological Museum renders the majestic figure of Zeus as he raises his right arm to throw the thunderbolt.

The eagle was the bird sacred to Zeus, since its wild indomitable nature reflected the power and autocratic character of the god; just as the eagle flies high and sees what is happening on the earth, so Zeus had his eyes fixed untiringly on the world that he ruled.

Zeus took as his queen Hera, one of the daughters of Kronos

1

3

2

2. Olympian Zeus. (Silver tetradrachm of Alexander the Great, Dion, Archaeological Museum.)

3. The abduction of the young Ganymede by Zeus. Zeus holds his travelling staff and Ganymede a cockerel, a love gift. The god was enchanted by the beauty of the young boy and abducted him to make him wine-pourer in his palace. (Terracotta group, 475-450 BC. Olympia, Archaeological Museum.)

177

1

gods, like Hermes and Dionysos, and several heroes, such as Herakles and Perseus.

The basic characteristic of Zeus was his complete omnipotence. Although he shared his authority with other gods, it was he who imposed order and no deity had the right to dispute his decisions. When Apollo protested about the unjust death of Asklepios, he was punished for his impiety. Similarly, no-one dared to censure Zeus for his infidelities, and even his own wife did not have the power to stop him; she could harm her rivals (such as Leto) or his children (such as Herakles), but not Zeus himself. The king of gods and men had complete control over his actions, and his aim was to impose order in the world and pass on his physical and psychological strength to as many descendants as possible.

and Rhea. The fruit of their marriage were Eileithyia, the goddess of childbirth, Ares, the god of war, Hebe, the goddess of youth, and Hephaistos, the god of metallurgy. Zeus also had many offspring from his relationships with other women, both mortal and immortal. He was the father of

2

1. Head of Zeus from a bronze statue in the sanctuary of the god at Olympia. (510-480 BC. Athens, National Archaeological Museum 6440.)

2. Thunderbolt inside a wreath. (Silver coin of Elis, 323-271 BC. Athens, Numismatic Museum.)

3. Zeus enthroned with his sceptre. (Amphora, 470-450 BC.British Museum.)

3

**The temple of Zeus at Olympia.
(c. 470-456 BC.)**

DIONYSOS

1

Dionysos was the son of Zeus and the beautiful Semele, daughter of Kadmos and Harmonia; like Athena, however, he was born from his father's body, because his mother died prematurely. The death of Semele was caused by Hera out of her jealousy when she realised that her husband had fallen in love with Semele and was going to her every evening, cloaking his majestic figure in darkness so as not to frighten her. Hera presented herself as a friend to her rival and persuaded her to ask her lover to reveal his identity. The young woman followed the goddess's advice, but could not bear the sight of Zeus's brilliance and expired as soon as she looked on him. Zeus at once took his unborn son from the body of his dead mistress and reared it himself in his thigh. When the period of pregnancy was over and Dionysos was born, his father concealed him for his safety until Hera's anger subsided.

The son of the unfortunate Semele became the god of wine, merry-making and the theatre. He it was who gave men the gift of wine and initiated them into its secrets. Appearing to a virtu-

1. Head of a statue of Dionysos. Probably from the west pediment of the temple of Apollo at Delphi. (c. 340-330 BC. Delphi Museum.)

2. Satyrs and maenads entertain Dionysos at a banquet, at which Hephaistos is arriving. (Hydria, c. 530-520 BC. British Museum B 302.)

3. Satyr and maenad. (Bronze mirror cover, 320-300 BC. Olympia, Archaeological Museum.)

2

ous citizen, Ikarios, who lived with his daughter, Erigone, in the deme of Ikaria in Attica (modern Dionysos), he gave him the vine and taught him how to make wine. The delighted Ikarios wished to share the gift of the god with other humans and gave the 'magical liquid' to a group of shepherds; unfortunately, however, he forgot to warn them about its effects; the shepherds, unaware of the symptoms of drunkenness, thought that Ikarios had tried to poison them, and killed him. Erigone died with him, hanging herself out of her grief. Since that time, wine has been served copiously at banquets and on festive occasions. It should be noted, however, that in the ancient world wine was not drunk 'neat' but was mixed with water

3

4. Marble statue of Dionysos from the small temple to him in the so-called 'Villa of Dionysos' at Dion. (Late 2nd c. AD. Dion, Archaeological Museum.)

4

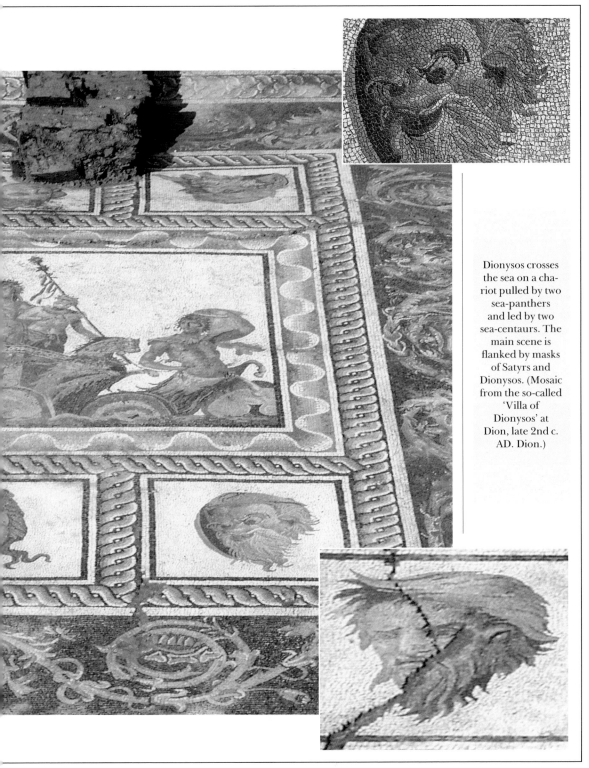

Dionysos crosses the sea on a chariot pulled by two sea-panthers and led by two sea-centaurs. The main scene is flanked by masks of Satyrs and Dionysos. (Mosaic from the so-called 'Villa of Dionysos' at Dion, late 2nd c. AD. Dion.)

1. Dionysos and Ariadne, accompanied by followers of Dionysos. (Bronze volute krater from Derveni. 330-310 BC. Thessaloniki Museum.)

2. Satyrs and maenads dance in a state of Dionysiac frenzy. (Terracotta plaque dedicated to the Nymphs. 525-500 BC. Delphi Museum.)

1

2

in the proportion 1:3 in large open vessels called kraters.

'Orgiastic' rituals were organised in honour of the patron god of merry-making. The god inspired men with Dionysiac frenzy and helped them, through dance and song, to escape from the routine of daily life and their earthly duties. The spirit of the god dominated the souls and mind of his followers, who answered his frenzied call and transcended themselves. From this Dionysiac belief in the transcending of the human 'nature' was born the theatre. Just as Dionysos spiritually dominates his followers, so the actor is dominated by the character he is playing; in both cases man succeeds in leaving behind his own personality and impersonating someone else. The priests of Dionysos were given honorary seats at all Greek theatres in memory of contribution made by the god to the birth of the actor's art.

Dionysos's symbols are the vine, from which wine is produced; the thyrsos, a sacred rod crowned with vine leaves and ivy; the kantharos, a drinking vessel in which wine is served; and the pelt of a panther, the animal sacred to the god.

Dionysos's retinue is called a thiasos (troupe) and consists of satyrs and maenads. Satyrs are monstrous beings, who are men from the waist up and goats from the waist down. The maenads, under the influence of Dionysiac frenzy seek to embody the god himself. Dancing in a state of ecstasy they hunt in the forests and eat their victims raw, believing they can see Dionysos before them.

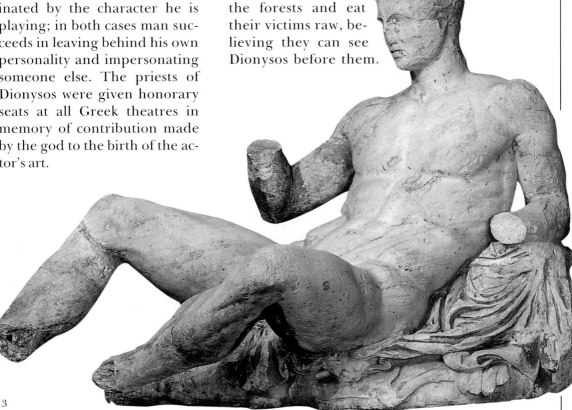

3. Male figure seated on an animal skin, probably Dionysos. (From the east pediment of the Parthenon, 447-432 BC. British Museum.)

3

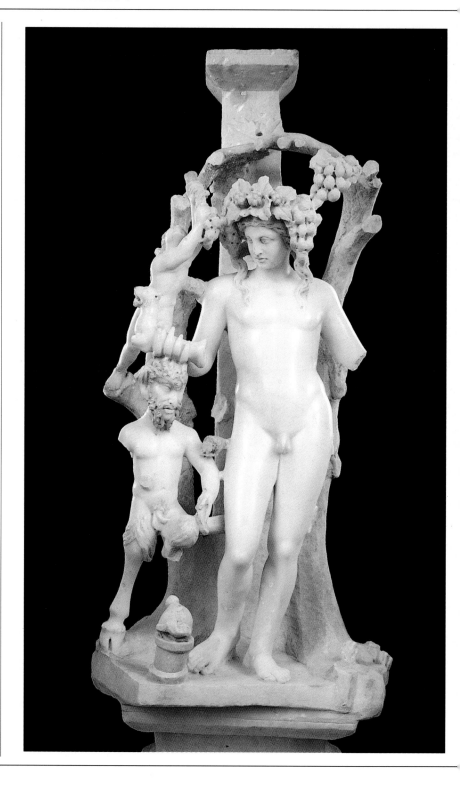

Dionysos, crowned with vine leaves and ivy, accompanied by Pan and a Satyr. (Table support, AD 170-180. Athens, National Archaeological Museum 5706.)

On a hydria in the British Museum (see p. 182) Dionysos lies on a couch and holds a kantharos, with vine-leaves depicted in the background. A satyr entertains him by playing the kithara and another dances to the rhythm of his music, accompanied by a maenad.

The god of wild merry-making could not settle in one place and travelled continuously with his followers, spreading his cult to mankind. During his wanderings he encountered many women to whom he was attracted; one of these was Ariadne, the daughter of Minos, whom Theseus abandoned on Naxos in order to satisfy Dionysos's desire. The sacred couple is depicted in divine majesty on a bronze krater from Derveni in Macedonia (see p. 186).

The meeting of Ariadne and Dionysos on Naxos. (Mosaic floor from the town of Chania. 3rd c. AD.)

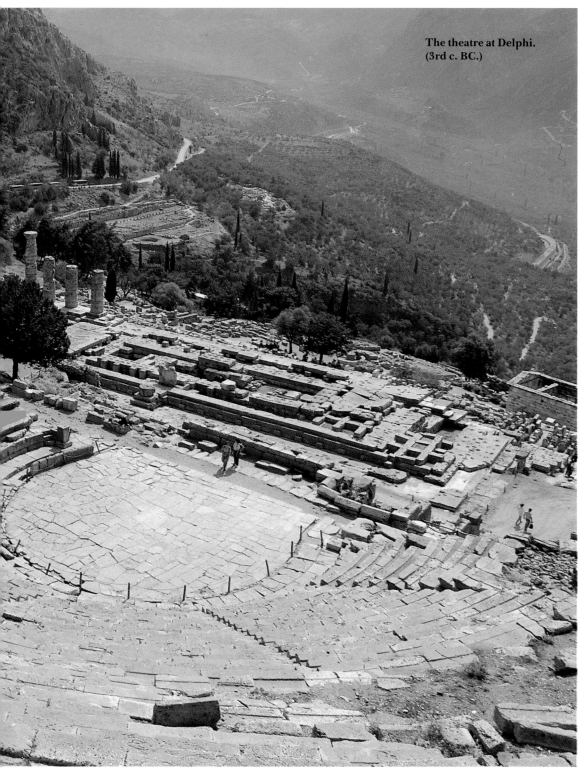

The theatre at Delphi. (3rd c. BC.)

HERMES
AND OTHER DIVINE MESSENGERS

1

ermes was the son of Zeus and Maia, daughter of the Titan Atlas who supported the vault of heaven on his shoulders. His lively character became evident at a very early age, and he lived free in nature, amusing himself by deceiving the gods and men through his cunning. It is to this spirit of play that the invention of the lyre is owed; Hermes made it from the shell of a tortoise, but later gave it as a reconciliation present to Apollo, the talented god of music, receiving in return the capacity of patron god of shepherds and their flocks.

Hermes was above all, however, the trusty messenger of the gods; he it was who carried their messages and performed a variety of missions. It was to him that Zeus assigned the task of taking Athena, Hera and Aphrodite to Troy to meet Paris-Alexander, who was to decide which of the three was the

1. Hermaic stele. (c. 2nd c. BC. Rhodes, Archaeological Museum.)

2. Hermes and the Graces. (Votive relief, 520-500 BC Athens, Acropolis Museum.)

2

most beautiful and should receive the apple of Eris (see pp. 108-110).

The messenger of the gods travelled from the higher regions of the heavens down to the deepest depths of the earth, taking not only messages, but also the souls of the dead to the gloom of Hades; Hermes Psychopompos escorted the souls to the gates of the Underworld or handed them over to Charon who took them in his boat to their last residence.

He was also the god of trade and travel, because the missions that he undertook obliged him to be continuously on the move and travel from one end of the earth to the other. Hermes was the patron god of travellers and cared for the security of the roads, which is why the Athenians set up rectangular marble pillars crowned with busts of

3. The Hermes of Praxiteles. The messenger of the gods holds the young Dionysos on his arm. (Marble statue, c. 330 BC. Olympia, Archaeological Museum.)

1. Iris, the winged messenger of the gods. (Kylix, c. 500 BC. Berlin, Staatliche Museen F 2278.)

2. Hermes wearing a petasos, himation and sandals. (Marble statue, Kos, Archaeological Museum.)

2

Hermes, which were called Hermaic stelai or herms, to mark the most important streets of their city. The god was also worshipped as patron god of the house with the epithet (Hermes) Propylaios, and small marble stelai were erected in front of the doors of houses in his honour. Hermes carried out his missions successfully, winning the trust of gods and the respect of men; at the same time, however, he was patron god of cheats and thieves, because it amused him to play tricks on mortals and immortals alike.

The main symbol of Hermes is the caduceus, a staff that indicated his capacity as bearer of messages and herald of events; in order to move very swiftly he wears a pair of winged boots and a winged hat, the petasos. In some cases, the god also holds the lyre, reminding us that it was he who invented this musical instrument, which became the symbol of the talent of Apollo.

We may note that Hermes was successor to Iris, who was the

first messenger of the gods. When Zeus assigned the role of the herald to his young son, Iris retained her capacity as mediator between the immortals, and it was she who went to Mount Olympos to tell Eileithyia that Leto was suffering badly from birth pains and take her to Delos.

In art, Iris is depicted winged, holding a caduceus, and wearing winged boots; she had the reputation of being able to travel to the ends of the earth, which is why the colours of the rainbow, the ends of which disappear over the horizon, are in Greek called 'the colours of Iris'.

3

3. Hermes with the caduceus, petasos, winged boots and lyre. (Drawing from a kalyx krater, c. 480 BC. Basel BS 482.)

4

5

4. Hermes watches the birth of Pandora. (Volute krater, c. 440 BC. Oxford 525.)

5. Hermes takes Herakles to Mount Olympos. (Kylix, c. 500 BC. Berlin, Staatliche Museen F 2278.)

HERA

Hera was the queen of Mount Olympos: the daughter of Kronos and Rhea, she was chosen by Zeus as his wife, after he established his rule over the world. Their wedding was celebrated with great brilliance and was honoured by all the gods. The wife of the father of gods and men embodied the ideal woman, and was the goddess of marriage and the family who protected lawful wives and their children.

The infidelities of Zeus, however, frequently disturbed her own marriage. Hera continually monitored her husband's move-

1. Zeus and Hera hold royal sceptres. (Kylix, c. 430 BC British Museum E 82.)

3

2

2. Hera with royal crown and sceptre.
(Drawing from a lekythos,
c. 470 BC. Basel, Ehel Collection.)

ments, and her proverbial jealousy often drove her to extremes. To avenge herself on Zeus she passionately persecuted his mistresses: Semele was killed and Leto tortured, for example, and she treated his illegitimate offspring with the same remorseless hatred, especially Herakles.

She herself bore Zeus four children: Eileithyia, the patron goddess of women in childbirth, Ares, the god of War, Hebe, the goddess of youth, who married Herakles and Hephaistos, the god of metallurgy. She drove

3. Head of a statue of Hera from her sanctuary at Argos.
(c. 420 BC. Athens, National Archaeological Museum 1571.)

1. Female head, probably of Hera. (Silver coin - stater - of Elis, 343-325 BC. Athens, Numismatic Museum.)

2. Head of Hera. The name of the goddess is inscribed on the band tying her hair. (Silver coin - stater - of Elis, 421-385 BC. Athens, Numismatic Museum.)

Hephaistos from Mount Olympos, because she was ashamed of his ugly appearance, and obliged him to live far from the other gods. Hephaistos survived alone by exploiting his innate talent, but he never forgave his mother for her harshness, and as soon as a suitable opportunity presented itself, he took his revenge on her. When he undertook to make two royal thrones for the palace of his parents, he seized the chance to humiliate his mother through an ingenious device: he fixed iron chains to the throne intended for Hera and covered them with elegant decoration, so that they could not be seen. As soon as the goddess sat down the chains wrapped themselves around her body and held her fast. Nobody could set her free from her bonds except Hephaistos himself. Despite the fact that all the other gods tried to persuade him to take pity on his mother, he was intransigent. In the end, Dionysos managed to deceive him by giving him wine to drink and taking him drunk to Mount Olympos. Hephaistos was then compelled to give way, but in return he asked for the beautiful Aphrodite as his wife (see pp. 167-168). This episode is depicted on the François vase in Florence: Zeus and Hera sit on their elaborate thrones, but the goddess is bound by the precious gift from her son. The royal couple, together with Athena, Ares, Artemis, Poseidon, Hermes and Aphrodite, wait anxiously for Hephaistos. The god appears at the top on a mule, accompanied by Dionysos and his followers, the satyrs and maenads, who are carrying wine flasks and dancing to the accompaniment of the flute.

4

In art Hera is recognised by the symbols of her high status: the royal sceptre and crown.

3.Hephaistos arrives on Olympos accompanied by Dionysos. (Volute krater, c. 570 BC. Florence 4209.)

4. Pair of gods, probably Zeus and Hera. (Metope from Temple E at Selinos, 460-450 BC. Palermo Museum.)

The Temple of Hera at Olympia. (c. 600 BC.)

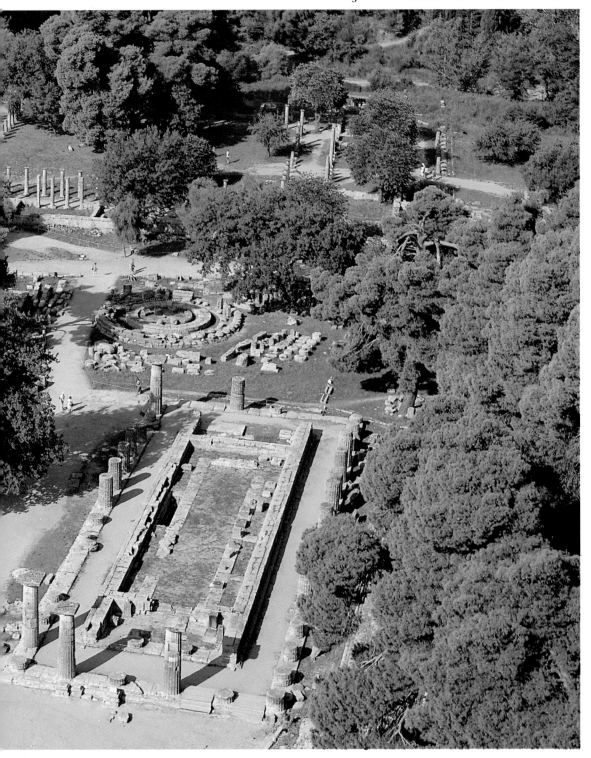

HEPHAISTOS

The royal couple of Zeus and Hera did not love all their children; they threw the new-born Hephaistos out of Olympos, and he was injured as he fell to earth and remained forever lame and a cripple. This rejection of Hephaistos by his parents is accounted for by various versions of the myth: Zeus is said to have punished Hephaistos because he found him plotting with Hera against him, or his mother is said not to have wanted him because she had conceived him against her wishes. According to a third version, however, Hephaistos had a genetic deformity which gave his mother a very difficult delivery. Hera was ashamed of this and sought to hide her shame by driving him away from her.

Hephaistos stood out because of his ugliness amongst the twelve Olympian gods, whose beauty was radiant; in the world of the immortals, he embodied the deformities and imperfections of mortals. However, his physical weaknesses were balanced by his great skill, for he was an excellent craftsman and therefore established himself as the god of metallurgy. He discovered how to melt metals on fire, which he took from the volcanic mountains of Lemnos or from Mount Etna on Sicily, where he had set up his workshop. Athena, the patron goddess of the arts, worked with

1. Hephaistos arrives on Olympos accompanied by Dionysos. (Volute krater, c. 570 BC. Florence 4209.)

Hephaistos
(Kylix, c. 430 BC.
Berlin, Staatliche
Museen
F 2537.)

him, and it was from their joint workshop that Prometheus stole fire to give to mankind.

Hephaistos made the weapons of Achilles, which the hero gave to Patroklos in order to check the Trojans when they were threatening the Achaian camp. After the death of Patroklos, Thetis again turned to Hephaistos to replace her son's weapons, before he entered battle to gain vengence for the death of his friend. On an amphora in Boston, the Nereid is in the workshop of the god of metallurgy to receive the famous weapons: the helmet and greaves are shown hanging on the wall behind the figures, and Hephaistos is still working on the shield, the elaborate scenes on which are described in great detail by Homer in the Iliad.

In sculpture and vase-painting Hephaistos is depicted leaning on a staff and holding his tools, the symbols that reveal his identity: the tongs were used by the god to work bronze and other metals in kilns heated to great temperatures, while the hammer, saw and chisel helped him to shape his elaborate creations.

3. Hermes and a satyr take Hephaistos, on horseback, to his mother Hera. (Kalyx krater, c. 490 BC. Louvre G 162.)

POSEIDON
AND OTHER GODS OF THE SEA

Poseidon was the son of Kronos and Rhea; when his brother, Zeus, dethroned their father, he made Poseidon god of the sea and assigned to him rule over the oceans, rivers, lakes and springs.

The symbol of authority of the god of the sea is the trident, just as the sceptre is the symbol of Zeus. Poseidon's trident, however, was also a very powerful weapon; the god used it to attack his enemies, and also to agitate the peaceful sea. Poseidon was renowned for his sharp

1. Poseidon and Amphitrite seated on banquet couches. (Kylix, c. 430 BC. British Museum E 82.)

temper, and both mortals and immortals trembled at his anger. During the Battle of the Giants, he fought courageously against the enemy; so great was his anger that he uprooted a whole island (Nisyros) and threw it at them, thereby turning them to route. Sailors always tried to win his favour to secure a safe voyage; they were well aware that with a single movement of his trident the god could stir up the seas and send travellers to their deaths.

Poseidon's sacred animal was the horse, because he created it and then gave it to mankind. The god was also father of Pegasos, the powerful winged horse of Bellerophon, which was born from the head of Medusa.

The horse and water were the two gifts offered by the god to the Athenians in order to be recognised as patron of their city, but they chose the sacred olive of Athena. Nevertheless, Poseidon was indirectly connected with the myths of Attica as the divine father of Theseus. Poseidon's gifts were also rejected by the inhabitants of Argos, who chose Hera as their patron. The god's offerings to mortals were in the end duly appreciated by the city of Isthmos, where

2. Marble statue of Poseidon from Milos. In his right hand he will have been holding the trident. (c. 150-130 BC. Athens, National Archaeological Museum 235.)

2

1. Poseidon at the assembly of the gods depicted on the east frieze of the Parthenon. 447-432 BC. (Athens, Acropolis Museum.)

2. Poseidon abducts Amphitrite, while her sisters, the Nereids, run in confusion and Triton reports the event to the girl's mother, Doris. (Drawing from a pyxis, c. 460 BC. Athens, National Archaeological Museum 1708.)

1

the Isthmian games, a great pan-Hellenic festival of athletic competitions, were held every four years in his honour.

The Nereid Amphitrite captivated Poseidon with her beauty, and the god decided to win her; the girl yielded to the god's amorous siege and followed him to become queen in his palace, which was in the dark depths of the sea. The fruit of their love was the Triton, a sea god who was a human from the waist upwards and a fish from the waist down. Triton's double form refers both to the divinity of his father and to the origins of his mother: Amphitrite's father was Nereus, one of the earliest sea gods, and her mother was Doris, a nymph of rivers and lakes and daughter of the Titan Okeanos, who ruled the seas and the rivers in the days when Kronos was lord of the world.

As we have already seen, Poseidon was one of the most important and powerful gods in ancient Greek mythology. This is confirmed even by the geographical position of Greece: since the social and economic

3

development of the country depended directly upon water, Poseidon's favour must have been of immense value to the success of any commercial or military enterprise, which inevitably involved travel over the sea.

3. Athena and Poseidon in conversation. (Amphora, c. 540-530 BC. Paris, Bibliothèque Nationale, Cabinet des Medailles et d'Antiquités 222.)

2

The temple of Poseidon at Sounion. (440-430 BC.)

OTHER MYTHICAL FIGURES
THE AMAZONS

The Amazons were a group of warlike women who lived in the city of Themiskyra on the Black Sea. They had created an independent society formed exclusively of women, who were distinguished by their courage and pride. They kept company with men only in order to bear children; they killed their male offspring and

1. Statue of an Amazon on horseback. (From the west pediment of the temple of Asklepios at Epidauros, c. 395-375 BC. Athens, National Archaeological Museum 136.)

brought up their girls to learn the arts of war. The principles and laws of the normal societies of the ancient Greek world were radically different from the way of life of the Amazons; we may therefore conclude that for the ancient Greeks the Amazons represented a barbarous, uncivilised race.

The most popular battles of the Amazons in Greek mythology involve Herakles and Theseus. We have already seen that one of the labours of Herakles was to get for Eurystheus the girdle that Ares had given to his daughter, Hippolyta, the Amazon queen. According to one version, Herakles faced the powerful army of the Amazons with the support of many other heroes, including Theseus. In the end the Amazons were defeated and the hero managed to snatch the precious girdle. During this conflict Theseus was entranced by the Amazon Antiope and decided to take her with him to Athens (see p. 99); others, indeed, say that their feelings were mutual and Antiope followed him willingly. Her action brought dishonour on the rest of the Amazons, who entertained a deadly hatred for men; they therefore decided to reassemble their army and launch an expedition against the Athenians.

The Amazon army soon ap-

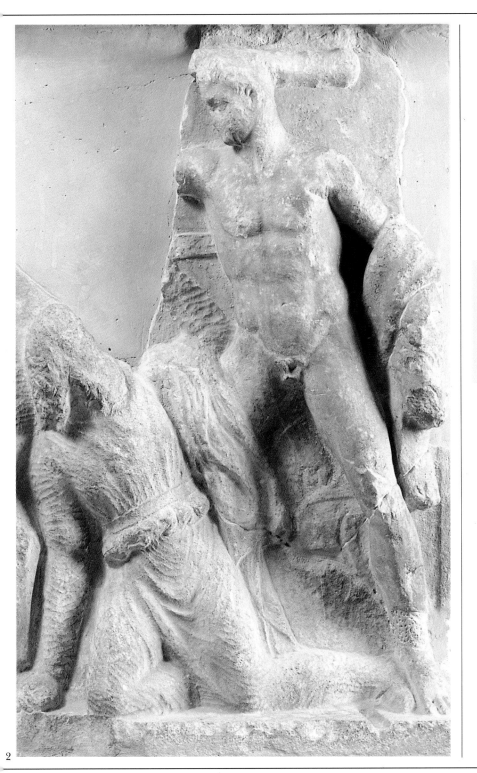

2. Herakles and
an Amazon.
(Frieze slab, 1st c.
AD. Delphi
Museum.)

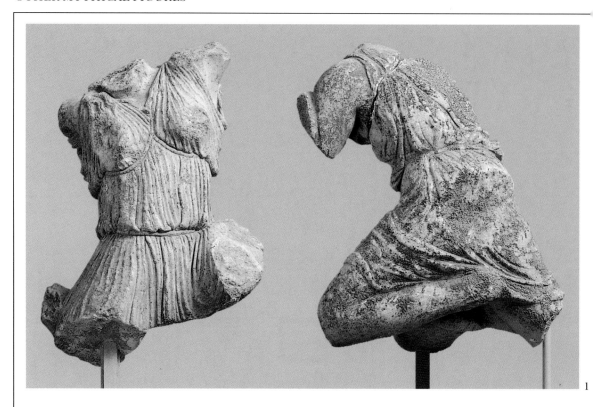

1

1. Statues of Amazons. (From the outer metopes of the Tholos at Delphi. 380-370 BC. Delphi Museum.)

peared menacingly before the walls of Athens. Theseus courageously defended his kingdom and in the end overcame the danger, but his beloved Antiope was killed on the field of battle. A scene from the conflict is depicted on a dinos in the British Museum: Theseus, accompanied by Peirithoos, wearing full panoply, attacks an Amazon who has fallen to the ground, while three mounted Amazons ride up to defend her.

The myth of the defeat of the Amazons at Athens promotes Theseus as a worthy king, and also glorifies the city itself, which successfully resisted a powerful army in order to maintain its independence. We may conjecture, therefore, that the Amazons symbolised all barbarian foes who threatened the security of the Greek cities. For the Athenians of the 5th century BC, the Battle of the Amazons probably had reference to a specific enemy, also of eastern origins: the Persians. In 490 BC, the Athenian army defeated the Persians at Marathon, and in 480 BC, the Persian army invaded Athens. The ultimate victory of the Greeks in the Persian Wars was due in large measure to the contribution of the Athenians; the sudden upsurge in the popularity of the myth of the Battle of the Amazons in the decoration of monuments constructed in Attica during the second half of the 5th century BC

2. The Battle of the Amazons. (Slab from the decoration of a grave monument, c. 350 BC. Athens, National Archaeological Museum 3614.)

3. The clash of Theseus and the Amazons outside the walls of Athens. (Dinos, c. 450 BC. British Museum 1899.7-21.5.)

was probably due to the memory of this event. (The Battle of the Amazons is one of the subjects depicted in the sculptures of the temple of Ares in the Ancient Agora, and also in the temple of Athena Nike and the Parthenon on the Acropolis.)

ASKLEPIOS

Asklepios was the son of Apollo and Koronis from Thessaly. His mother is said to have given birth to him at Epidauros, however, and later to have abandoned him to rid herself of the shame of having born an illegitimate child. He was brought up by his father, who taught him the secrets of medicine and sent him to the Centaur Cheiron on Pelion for his education.

Asklepios was a famous expert in and teacher of medicine; he had the gift of being able to heal all kinds of illnesses and to relieve men of their pain. His popularity, however, was also the cause of his death. The rumour that Asklepios was even able to raise the dead perturbed Zeus, who naturally did not wish men's belief in his own omnipotence to be shaken; the only solution was to put an end to Asklepios's life, and he therefore threw his thunderbolt and killed him. Embittered at the unjust death of his son, Apollo attempted to take vengeance on the Kyklops who had made the deadly weapon

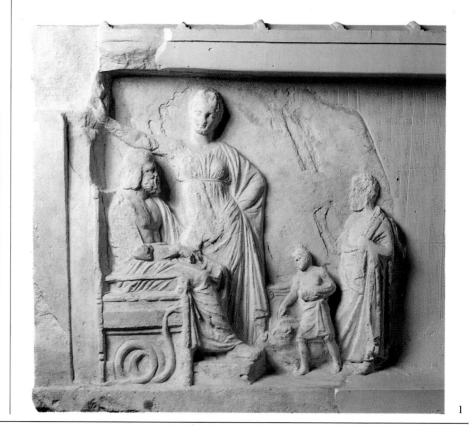

1. Asklepios, seated on a throne, accompanied by Hygeia, receives the offerings of his worshippers. (Votive relief, c. 350 BC. Athens, National Archaeological Museum 1330.)

1

thrown by Zeus. No-one, however, had the right to dispute the decisions of the father of gods and men and whoever violated this rule must be punished: Apollo paid for his impious act by serving Admetos, the king of Thessaly, for one year.

The work of Asklepios was continued by his children, Machaon, Podaleirios, Iaso, Panakeia and Akeso, who had been taught the secrets of medicine by their father, and also by his wife Hygeia.

After his death, Asklepios was honoured as a god. The most important of his sanctuaries was founded in Epidauros in the early 5th century BC, and thousands of believers from different parts of Greece flocked to it to be healed. The pilgrims first sacrificed to the god and took part in purification rituals, which prepared them physically and spiritually to enter the *enkoimeterion*, the sacred building where the god appeared to them in their dreams and told them the appropriate remedy for their complaint. Asklepios cured simpler illnesses while the sick person was asleep, but

3

2.Asklepios, wearing a himation and bearded, leans on a staff up which a snake is coiling itself. (Marble statue, 4th c. BC. Athens, National Archaeological Museum.)

3.Head of Hygeia from a marble statue of the goddess. (c. 360 BC. Athens, National Archaeological Museum 3602.)

2

1

1. The daughters of Asklepios. (Marble statues, 2nd c. AD. Dion, Archaeological Museum.)

2. Marble statue of Asklepios. (3rd c. AD. Rhodes, Archaeological Museum.)

2

the more serious cases were assigned to his priests, who carried out the course of treatment prescribed by him.

The cult of Asklepios was brought to Attica during the Peloponnesian War (431-404 BC), when the population of the city was being decimated by illness and injury. The priest Telemachos brought Asklepios, in the form of a snake from Epidauros to the city of Athens in 420-419 BC, where his sanctuary was founded beneath the Acropolis.

Large numbers of votive reliefs have been discovered in the sanctuaries of Asklepios, offered in gratitude by the faithful towards their benefactor-god. The simplest of these depict only the specific part of body that was in need of therapy, and are in some ways reminiscent of modern *ex votos*. In monumental compositions, the god himself watches the procession of the pilgrims and accepts their offerings. A typical example is formed by a relief in the Athens National Ar-

4

chaeological Museum from the Asklepieion in this city: Asklepios is seated on a throne, around which his sacred symbol, the snake, is coiled, and next to him stands Hygeia followed by worshippers. The gods are distinguished from the mortals by their imposing size, as usual in votive reliefs in the ancient world.

3

3. Podaleirios, one of the sons of Asklepios. (Marble statue, 2nd c. AD. Dion, Archaeological Museum.)

4. The arrival of Asklepios on Kos. (Mosaic, 3rd c. AD. Kos Museum.)

5. Hygeia with the sacred snake of Asklepios. (Marble statue, 3rd c. AD. Rhodes, Archaeological Museum.)

5

EUROPA
HER FOREBEARS AND DESCENDANTS

The continent of Europe is named after a princess who was born in Asia, but whose descent was from the Argolid. One of Europa's ancestors was Io, the daughter of Inachos, the king of Argos, who had been obliged to flee from her homeland because of the hatred of Hera. The goddess was angered when she learned of the affair between the beautiful Io and omnipotent Zeus, and took her revenge by turning Io into a cow, setting all-seeing Argos (who had eyes all over his body) to guard her. Even when Hermes killed Argos, Hera devised another way of punishing Io: she sent a gadfly to chase her continually, compelling her to run in despair from place to place. It was only when she came to Egypt that Io again assumed the form of a woman and was able to bear the child that Zeus had given to her. Her son, Epaphos became king in his native land and had a daughter, Libya.

Europa was the granddaughter of Libya, and daughter of Agenor and Telephassa, who ruled in Asia and had three more children: Kilix, Kadmos and Phoenix.

Agenor's family lived happily until Zeus fell in love with his

1. Zeus, transformed into a bull, carries Europa over the sea. (Hydria, c. 370 BC. British Museum E 231.)

2. Europa on the bull. (Poros metope from the 'monopteral' building at Delphi, 590-580 BC. Delphi Museum.)

beautiful daughter. The god turned himself into a bull and approached the girl when she was playing happily with her friends in the fields. The bull was so gentle that it did not frighten the girls and as it was amusing them with its games, Europa innocently sat on its back. The god did not miss this opportunity, but at once rose up into the air and went off taking Europa with him. Travelling over land and sea he brought her to Crete, which he had chosen as the place to couple with her; there Europa brought up their offspring, Minos and Rhadamanthys. The god also ensured that his beloved married the king of Crete, Asterios, so that his children should not grow up without a father.

As was to be expected, the sons of Europa inherited the throne of their adoptive father. When the time came, however, for them to claim the kingdom of Crete, the two men quarrelled. Minos asserted that it was the will of the gods that he should become king and prayed for a divine sign to prove the truth of his words. His request was answered by Poseidon who sent a bull from the sea, on condition that it should be sacrificed in his honour. Rhadamanthys stayed with his brother and assumed responsibility for legal and juridical matters, because he was famous for his sound judgement and sense of justice. We may note that Minos also possessed similar virtues, and after their deaths, the two brothers were appointed eternal judges of souls in Hades.

During the reign of Minos Crete developed into a major

power in the Mediterranean. Minos organised the economy of the island around the strong palaces of Knossos and Phaistos, passed laws, developed shipping, trade and the arts, and secured peace and prosperity for his subjects.

Minos, however, neglected his promise to Poseidon and did not sacrifice the bull; to punish him, the god inspired in Minos's wife, Pasiphae, the daughter of Helios, an unnatural erotic desire for the sacred beast. To fulfil her desire, the queen sought the assistance of Daidalos; Daidalos was a famous Athenian craftsman who had been exiled from Athens and had fled to Crete, where he won the confidence of Minos, and had undertaken the construction of palaces and other buildings. Daidalos offered his services to the queen by making a perfect wooden cow, into which Pasiphae entered and coupled with the bull. From their union was born the Minotaur, a monstrous being with the body of a man and head of a bull, who lived in the famous labyrinth and was fed human flesh. The Minotaur was eventually killed by Theseus, but Poseidon's anger gradually drove the king to his death. Minos decided to punish Daidalos for his ingratitude, assembled his fleet and began to look for him throughout

1. Europa crosses the sea on the sacred bull. (Mosaic from the Casa Romana on Kos 3rd c. AD.)

1

2. Europa holds on to the bull's horn. (Bell krater, c. 490 BC. Tarquinia, Museo Nazionale RC 7456.)

2

the world. After much wandering, he was informed that Daidalos had taken refuge on Sicily, at the palace of Kokalos; Kokalos, however, refused to surrender his guest and killed Minos through a trick.

After the death of its glorious king, Crete gradually went into decline and the palaces were abandoned. Europa never returned to her country, but lived in Crete and when she died the inhabitants of the island honoured her as a goddess. Her brothers looked for her in many lands on the orders of their father, but failed to find her, and did not dare to return to their homes, out of shame. The three men settled down in different parts of the world, where they founded their own kingdoms: Kilix in Cilicia, Phoenix in Phoenicia and Kadmos in Kadmeia (Thebes).

JASON
AND THE ARGONAUT EXPEDITION

1-2. A warrior departs on an expedition. (Ivory plaque, c. 570 BC. Delphi Museum.)

K retheus, the son of Aiolos, the lord of the winds, had his palace at Iolkos in Thessaly. The family of Kretheus was divided after his death, because his second-born son, Pelias, usurped the throne from the first-born, Aison, the father of Jason.

When Aison lost his kingdom, he gave Jason to the Centaur Cheiron to protect him from his enemies. Jason grew up secure in the mountains of Pelion, exercising his mind and body under the leadership of the wise Centaur. When the first two decades of his life had been completed, he decided to return to Iolkos to claim the kingdom that had been usurped by his father's brother.

Jason's arrival at Iolkos was from the very first an event of ill omen for Pelias. The youth en-tered the city wearing only one sandal, because he had lost the other on his journey. Pelias was terrified at this apparently insignificant detail, because he remembered the oracle that had warned him that he would lose his life at the hands of a 'one-sandalled man'. In order to keep his throne, and indeed his very life, Pelias decided to assign an impossible task to Jason: to claim his father's throne, the hero had to bring the golden fleece from the sacred grove of Ares in Kolchis, the country ruled by Aietes. First he had to succeed in crossing the ocean separating Thessaly from Kolchis and then seize the golden fleece from the fearsome serpent that guarded it.

It was a long journey and a very difficult mission, and the hero therefore had to secure a stout boat and able companions. Fate began to smile on Jason from the moment that Athena took his part. The goddess asked the famous craftsman Argo to make a swift ship for fifty oarsmen, and she herself oversaw the work. In a very short time the beautiful ship Argo, as it was called after its maker, was ready and Jason had to find a crew for it. The fifty young men that accompanied him were called Argonauts and their mission the Argonaut expedition. As in Herakles' expedition against the Amazons and the hunt for the Kalydonian boar, the most famous heroes from all over Greece took part in the Argonaut expedition: Herakles from Boeotia, Theseus from Athens, Amphiaraos from Argos, the Dioskouroi from Sparta, Meleager from Kalydon, Peleus from Thessaly, Kalais and Zetes, the sons of Boreas, the god of the north wind, and many oth-

ers. Orpheus from Thrace kept time for the oarsmen with his enchanting music and calmed the sea with his singing: in the scene on a metope at Delphi, Orpheus with his lyre, together with another musician and two horsemen (possibly the Dioskouroi) are boarding the Argo (see p. 226).

As they crossed the Aegean sea, the Argonauts stopped at various places and faced many dangers. In Thrace they encountered king Phineus, who had blinded his two sons, because he believed the lies told him by

3. The Argo and the Argonauts. (Drawing from the scene on a volute krater, c. 400-330 BC. Ruvo, Museo Jatta 1501).

3

1

2

1. The sons of Boreas chase off the Harpies to rescue Phineus from his torment. (Gold and ivory relief, c. 570 BC. Delphi Museum.)

2. Orpheus and other musicians sing to accompany the journey of the Argonauts. (Metope from the 'monopteral' temple at Delphi, 590-580 BC. Delphi Museum.)

succeeded in ploughing a field using two divine fire-breathing bulls; after this he had to sow the teeth of a serpent and kill the Giants who would spring from them. The hero began to despair, but the gods once again offered him their support by firing arrows of love at Aietes' daughter, Medea, who knew the secrets of magic. The young girl, blinded by her love for Jason, decided to use her cunning and potions to help him. Having given him her magic ointment to protect him from the breath of the bulls, she told him to throw a stone amongst the giants in order to make them kill each other.

When Jason had successfully completed this difficult labour, Aietes refused to keep his promise, and in order to retain possession of the golden fleece tried to burn the Argo. Nothing could stand in the way of the

their stepmother. For this act of injustice Phineus had been harshly punished by Zeus. The god condemned him to lose his sight and sent the Harpies, winged female deities, to torture him by stealing his food. Kalais and Zetes freed Phineus from his torture by driving off the Harpies; in return he gave the Argonauts instructions on how they could safely reach their destination, and sent favourable winds for their voyage. The episode is depicted on a gold and ivory plaque in the Delphi Museum. The two Harpies run of with Phineus's food, pursued by the two sons of Boreas; of the figure of the king, only part of the arm is preserved, which can be seen above the table.

Following the advice of Phineus, the Argonauts came to Kolchis. Their adventures had not come to an end, however. Aietes did not agree to give them the golden fleece, but to avoid a conflict, set certain conditions. He agreed to meet their demand if Jason hero, however, who had the gods on his side. Medea led Jason to the grove of Ares and helped him to get the golden fleece by putting the serpent to sleep with one of her magic potions. After this she did not hesitate to kill one of her own brothers, in order to delay her father's soldiers and give the Argonauts the chance to get away from Kolchis. Medea followed Jason and his companions and helped them in many adventures on their return voyage. Jason valued the dedication of the young woman and made her his wife.

When the Argonauts returned in triumph to Iolkos, Pelias refused to keep his promise. The god's oracle, however, was fated to prove true. To punish Pelias, Medea gave his daughters a magic potion and persuaded them that they would be able to make their father young again if they cut him to pieces and boiled him in it. The women followed the witch's instructions, and killed Pelias with their own hands.

Jason assigned rule at Iolkos to Pelias's son, Akastos, and himself set off with his family for Corinth, the kingdom inherited by Aietes from Helios. Medea, as a child of Aietes, was welcomed at Corinth and lived there happily for ten years with her husband and children. Their marriage, however, had a dramatic end; Jason fell in love with an-

3

other woman and Medea, having taken vengeance on him by killing their children, was exiled from her country for the second time.

3. Jason seizes the golden fleece. (Krater, early 4th c. BC. Naples, Museo Nazionale Archeologico 3248.)

KADMOS
AND THE FOUNDATION OF THEBES

Kadmos kills the serpent at the Areia Spring. (Drawing from a Hydria, c. 420-410 BC. Berlin, Staatliche Museen F2634.)

K admos was the son of Agenor, who ruled in Asia. When Zeus abducted his sister, Europa, Kadmos and his brothers left their country to look for her at their father's orders. Kadmos came to Greece and visited many cities, which readily offered him hospitality. He took every opportunity of sacrificing to the gods and being of use to the inhabitants. According to a different version of the myth, indeed, in which Kadmos and Europa are the children of Phoenix, and not of Agenor, it was Kadmos who taught the Greeks the alphabet, which is based on the Phoenician script.

In his travels from place to place, Kadmos came to the oracle at Delphi and asked Apollo to reveal to him where his sister was. The god advised him to follow the sacred cow that would appear before him; this would show him the proper place for him to settle and found his kingdom. The heaven-sent animal stopped in Boeotia, near Thebes.

In order to establish his rule over this area, however, Kadmos had first to carry out a labour: to kill the deadly serpent sent by

Ares to rule over the only source of water in land, which was called the Areia Spring. No-one had ever survived the attacks of the terrible serpent, but Kadmos had Athena on his side; he weakened the monster by throwing stones at it and then rushed at it with his sword. On a hydria in the Hermitage Museum, a group of gods is watching the episode: the two rivals are depicted in the centre, and between them stand Athena, who is turned towards her favourite, and Nike, who is awarding a wreath as his prize; amongst the spectators can be recognised Poseidon, with his trident, Hermes, holding the caduceus, Demeter with the royal sceptre and Persephone with the torches of Eleusis, Apollo with a laurel branch, and Eros, who is placing a crown at the feet of Thebes, the locally honoured nymph. After the end of the struggle, Athena told Kadmos to plant the serpent's teeth in the ground, and the inhabitants of Thebes were born from them. Before the hero could assume power, however, he was obliged to enter the service of Ares for eight years, to propitiate the god for the murder of the serpent.

Having completed his service, Kadmos founded Kadmeia, the citadel that later developed into the famous city of Thebes. He took as his queen Harmonia, the daughter of Ares and Aphrodite. Their wedding was celebrated with great brilliance; Athena gave the bride an elaborate peplos and Aphrodite gave her daughter a valuable necklace, made by Hephaistos. The couple had five children: Semele, Agaue, Autonoe, Ino and Polydoros. All four daughters were fated to have dramatic ends.

The cause of the evil was Zeus's love for Semele, which incurred the deadly jealousy of Hera. The goddess killed the young girl while she still carried inside her Dionysos, who was then reared inside the thigh of his mighty father.

The birth of the illegitimate child enraged Hera even further. The next victim of her jealousy was Ino, Semele's sister, who had taken the young Dionysos into her family. To punish her, the goddess sowed dissension between her and her husband, Athamas; when Athamas killed

Dionysos travels with his retinue to spread his cult. (Amphora, c. 500-490 BC. Munich.)

their son, Learchos, in a frenzy of rage, Ino lost her sanity and, holding their other child, Melikertes, in her arms, jumped from the rocks and was killed. Out of compassion the gods turned them into sea gods and called them Leukothea and Palaimon.

Agaue was punished severely by Dionysos, because she disapproved of his mother's relationship with Zeus. The episode is narrated by Euripides in his famous tragedy the *Bacchae*. When Dionysos and his followers came to Thebes, to teach the secrets of his cult, the country was ruled by Pentheus, who was the son of Agaue and Echion, and successor of his grandfather, Kadmos. Because the god appeared to the Thebans in human form, the king and Agaue doubted his divine nature and refused to accept the worship of Dionysos. They decided, moreover, to arrest him and put him in prison, ignoring the sage advice of the venerable Kadmos and the prophet Teiresias. This act of impiety incurred the wrath of the god, who escaped from prison to demonstrate to all the irresistible force of his cult. Having entranced the Theban women with his spirit, he led them on to the slopes of Mount Kithairon, and in a state of frenzy, they danced and sang in the forests, hunting and tearing their victims apart, like maenads. Pentheus went to the mountain to find out precisely what had happened. There, however, the king fell victim to the women's madness, the leading role being played by his mother. Agaue killed her child with her own hands and then appeared in Thebes proudly holding his head. This dramatic image summed up the triumph of the worship of Dionysos, and the destruction of those who dared to dispute it.

The third daughter of Kadmos had an equally unfortunate end. Autonoe died from her grief for her son, Aktaion, the famous hunter killed by Artemis when she caught him secretly watching her at her toilet (see p. 161).

Finally, Polydoros had the fortune to succeed his father on the throne of Thebes. The young king married Nykteis and had a son, Labdakos. Labdakos was the founder of the Labdakidai and grandfather of Oedipus, whose name is linked with the dramatic events that led to the destruction of Thebes.

2. Aktaion is savaged by the dogs, at Artemis's orders. (Metope from temple E at Selinous, 460-450 BC. Palermo, National Museum.)

2

THE CENTAURS

1. Head of a Centaur. (From the west pediment of the temple of Zeus at Olympia, c. 470-456 BC. Olympia, Archaeological Museum.)

The Centaurs were descendants of Ixion who had ventured to declare his love for Hera, in disregard of her mighty husband. Zeus became aware of this and tested Ixion by sending him a cloud in the form of his wife. When Ixion succumbed to temptation, the god cast him down into Tartaros in his rage and condemned him to rotate eternally, bound to a wheel. From the union between Ixion and the cloud was born the Centaur that later became the founding father of all the other Centaurs. The fruit of such a union could naturally not be harmonious. The Centaurs developed into wild beings that caused destruction, threatening the peace and balance of human societies. They dwelt mainly in the forests of Thessaly, not respecting the laws or order. Their form reflected their nature: their bodies combined human features with those of a horse, and the long, unkempt beards framing their faces stressed their wildness still further.

Ixion's son Peirithoos, a half-brother of the Centaurs, ruled over the famous race of Lapiths in Thessaly. Peirithoos became a close friend of Theseus, and accompanied him on many of his adventures. Peirithoos invited Theseus to his wedding, where an unpleasant surprise awaited them. The wild Centaurs came down from the mountains in the area holding branches and tree-trunks, invaded the wedding ceremony, destroyed everything on the wedding table and then seized the bride and the wives of the guests, intending to carry them off. A fierce battle ensued, in which Theseus fought bravely alongside Perithoos and helped him to rescue his beloved. The episode is depicted on the west pediment of the temple of Zeus at Olympia, in which the violence of the clash and the wildness of the Centaurs is delineated with impressive realism.

Another incident involving the abduction of a woman involved the clash between Herakles and the Centaur Nessos (see p. 78).

Herakles was also associated with the death of Cheiron, the only wise Centaur, who lived in the forests of Mount Pelion, where he taught many of the heroes, in-

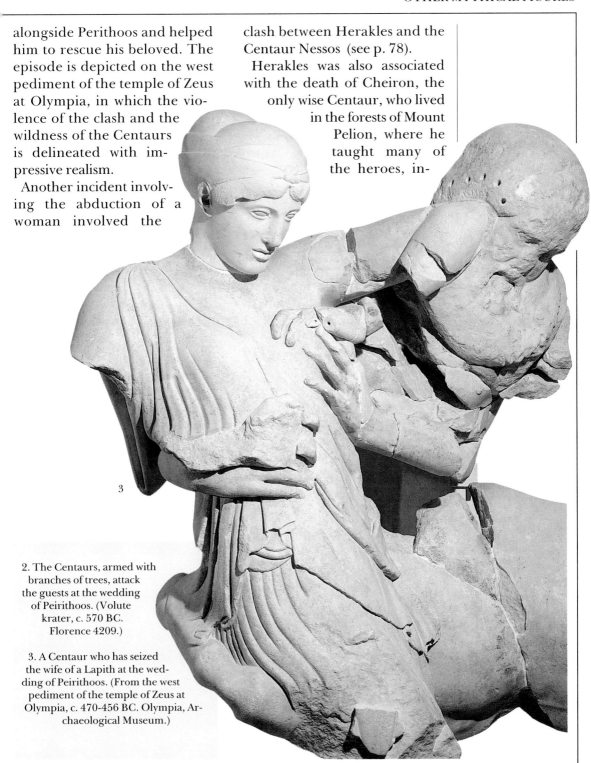

3

2. The Centaurs, armed with branches of trees, attack the guests at the wedding of Peirithoos. (Volute krater, c. 570 BC. Florence 4209.)

3. A Centaur who has seized the wife of a Lapith at the wedding of Peirithoos. (From the west pediment of the temple of Zeus at Olympia, c. 470-456 BC. Olympia, Archaeological Museum.)

1. Two Centaurs attempt to push the Lapith Kaineus into the earth, since he was invulnerable as long as he could keep his body above ground. (Bronze sheet, 650-625 BC. Olympia, Archaeological Museum.)

2. A Lapith tries tres to raise a stone to throw it at a Centaur. (From the north metopes of the Parthenon, c. 447-432 BC. British Museum.)

cluding Jason and Achilles. This episode began in Arkadia when the Centaur Pholos entertained Herakles in his cave, and to make him welcome decided to open a large pithos of wine, a gift from Dionysos that he kept buried in the ground. The smell of the wine affected the other Centaurs who became drunk and attacked Pholos and his guest. Herakles defended himself with his arrows, and some of the Centaurs escaped by running to the cave of Cheiron on Pelion. The hero pursued them in his wrath, but unwittingly killed the wise Centaur and Pholos with his poisoned arrows.

The wildness of the Centaurs and their isolation in the forests led to their being considered gods of nature. And it is true that, despite their human descent, their behaviour and way of life was more reminiscent of animal societies. Their dual appearance perhaps hints at the struggle between their human and horse natures; these coexisted harmoniously in the case of Cheiron, since he had the gift of wisdom, whereas in the other Centaurs the bestial instincts overcame reason.

The clash between men and Centaurs may be compared with the conflict between the gods and the Giants, since involved a clash between the forces of good and evil: the Giants were descendants of gods but revolted against Zeus to overthrow the order he had imposed on the world; and the Centaurs, despite being born of a mortal, refused to reconcile themselves to the laws and values that governed human societies. It might therefore be said that the both defeat of the Giants and the defeat of the Centaurs symbolise the victory of civilisation over anarchy.

2

3. The Battle of the Centaurs at the wedding of Peirithoos. At the centre is the dominating figure of Apollo, whose presence imposes order. (West pediment of the temple of Zeus at Olympia, c. 470-456 BC. Olympia, Archaeological Museum.)

3

MELEAGER
AND THE HUNT FOR THE
KALYDONIAN BOAR

Meleager was the son of Oineus and Althaia who ruled at Kalydon in Aetolia. When the Fates visited Meleager in his cradle, Klotho and Lachesis blessed him with beauty, courage and honour, while Atropos declared that his life would come to an end when a log on the fire that heated the child's room burned out. Althaia, however was listening secretly to their words and, as soon as they left, seized the piece of wood and concealed it in a chest. Meleager grew to manhood and became a handsome youth, famous for his courage and his hunting skills.

Meleager's life took a dramatic turn when his father neglected to offer the appropriate sacrifice to Artemis. In her anger, the goddess punished him by sending a boar to the city which cre-

ated terrible destruction in the fields and killed the people. The only way to propitiate Artemis was to slay the beast and sacrifice it in her honour. To this end, Oineus summoned the bravest young men from all over Greece and organised the famous hunt for the Kalydonian Boar. His son, Meleager, was an outstanding member of the group of hunters, though many other famous heroes also took part, amongst them the Dioskouroi – Kastor and Polydeukes – from Sparta and Amphiaraos from Argos, Peleus, Admetos, Jason, and Perithoos from Thessaly, Theseus from Athens, Iolos from Boeotia, Iphiklos and Plexippos – the brothers of Althaia – from Pleuron, and one woman, Atalanta, from Arkadia. The fact that the 'weaker' sex was represented on such a dan-

1. The hunt for the Kalydonian boar. (Volute krater, c. 570 BC. Florence 4209.)

gerous mission is strange, but Atalanta was no ordinary woman. Her father had abandoned her on the mountains when she was born, because she was not the male child that he desired; she was raised on the milk of a bear, however, and became truly indomitable. She shunned marriage and preferred to live free in the forests, engaged in hunting and athletics, was better than many men at wrestling, and was even more famous for her marksmanship as a huntress. She could not therefore be omitted from the group of youths who assembled to save Kalydon.

The king proclaimed that whoever succeeded in killing the Kalydonian boar would receive its pelt as a prize. This difficult, dangerous venture is depicted on the François Vase: the boar is at the centre of the scene, with a fallen hunter and his hound dead at its feet; he is being attacked frontally by two pairs of hunters with javelins, led by Meleager and Peleus and followed by Atalanta and Melanion, accompanied by a hunting dog and the archer Euthymachos; the main figures are flanked by many other hunters with raised javelins and bows. After many attempts Atalanta succeeded in wounding the boar, giving Meleager the chance to deliver the *coup de grâce*. Delighted at the outcome of the hunt and bewitched by

2

Atalanta, Meleager announced that he would award the prize for the contest to her. His decision, however, provoked a violent reaction on the part of his uncles, who were unable to accept that a woman should distinguish herself in this way amongst all the men. The disagreement led to a clash in which Meleager killed his mother's brothers. Althaia was badly shaken by the bad news and in her distress and grief sought to punish her son for his outrageous behaviour: she took the log of wood that she had kept hidden for so many years out of the chest and threw it onto the fire. Meleager died instantly and his unfortunate mother, regretting her action, followed the fate of her child.

Oineus later married Periboia and had a son, Tydeus, by her who was one of the seven generals that joined Polyneikes on his expedition against Thebes.

MEDEA

1

Medea, who is associated with the Argonaut expedition, was daughter of Aietes, and knew the secrets of magic. She betrayed her father and abandoned her country out of love for Jason. Medea helped her beloved to take the golden fleece from Kolchis, and followed him back to Greece, where she lived with him at Corinth. Jason, however, after ten years of marriage, became enchanted with Glauke, the daughter of Kreon, king of Corinth. The dramatic outcome of the legend is narrated by Euripides in his tragedy *Medea*.

When Medea learned that Jason was intending to abandon her, she tried to get him to change his mind by reminding him that she had left her homeland to follow him, and had none of her friends or relations around her to protect her. He refused to accept that she had made sacrifices for him, however, and said that the goddess of Love had wanted to save his life and had merely used her as a means of fulfilling this aim. To justify his decision, moreover, he advanced the excuse that he had chosen to marry Kreon's daughter in order to give his children the chance to grow up in a royal family. Medea, enraged at the accusations and excuses put forward by Jason, uttered dire threats and imprecations against him. Using this behaviour as an excuse, Kreon ordered that she should be exiled along with her children, in order to protect his daughter. In her bitterness, Medea decided to take the harshest revenge on those who had contributed to her misfortune. To gain time, Medea first approached Kreon and used gentle, flattering words to him; on the excuse that she needed a few hours to prepare herself for the journey, she persuaded him to allow her to stay in Corinth for one more day. She then took advantage of the visit of the king of Athens, Aigeus, and bound him by oath to support and protect her, after which she put her diabolical design into practice.

Medea first begged Jason to forgive her and to keep their children with him, sealing her words with two precious gifts, an elaborate dress and a gold crown, and expressing the wish that her sons should offer them to their new mother, so as to win her favour. She had covered these resplendent gifts with a deadly poison, however, and as soon as her rival put them on, she suffered terrible pain, her head caught fire from the crown and her body gradually melted. Her fate was shared by her father; seeing his daughter in torment, Kreon took her into his arms and his body stuck to hers.

The death of the young woman, however, was not the only punishment that Medea had devised to wound Jason. Determined to go to the bitter extreme, she raised her knife and took the lives of her own children, in order to remove from the world the fruit of their unhappy marriage. Jason attempt-

ed in vain to prevent this terrible crime. Medea left Corinth riding in the chariot given to her by her grandfather, Helios, and fled to Athens. There she became the wife of king Aigeus and gave him a son, Medos. She was finally exiled from Greece, however, when she attempted to poison Theseus, her husband's legitimate successor.

2. Medea kills one of her children before the statue of Apollo. (Amphora, c. 330-320 BC. Louvre K 300.)

2

ODYSSEUS

Odysseus, the famous king of Ithake, was son of Laertes and Antikleia. His wife was Penelope, by whom he had a son, Telemachos. In the *Iliad*, Homer describes Odysseus as one of the most charismatic of the Achaian leaders, distinguished by his courage and cunning, who makes a major contribution to the positive result of the expedition. The hero's return to Ithake, and his wanderings and adventures over a period of ten long years, are narrated by the poet in the epic *Odyssey*.

When Troy had finally fallen, and the 'fair Helen' had returned with Menelaos to Sparta, the victors set off home to their homelands. Odysseus gathered together his companions, put the spoils he had won on his ships, and set off for Ithake. The first port of call on the journey was the island of the Kikones, which he captured; he respected the priest of Apollo, however,

1. The blinding of Polyphemos. (Fragment of a krater, c. 660 BC. Argos, Archaeological Museum.)

2. Odysseus blinds the Kyklops with the aid of his companions. The Kyklops attempts to flee, while still holding the kylix containing the wine. (Amphora, c. 670 BC. Elefsina, Archaeological Museum.)

3. Odysseus escapes from the cave of the Kyklops bound under the belly of a sheep. (Bronze figurine, c. 575-525 BC. Delphi Museum.)

and in return the latter gave him valuable vases and utensils and twelve flasks of wine. A storm over the next days cast him up in the land of the Lotus-eaters, who cultivated the lotus flower; Odysseus rejected their hospitality, however, when he realised that anyone who ate the fruit of this plant forgot his homeland.

The wind then brought him to the land of the Kyklopes, where his many adventures began. According to Homer's account, the Kyklopes had only one eye in the middle of their forehead, were wild and lived a pastoral life, dwelling in caves and tend-ing their flocks. Odysseus and his comrades cast anchor off the land of the Kyklopes and went ashore to investigate, but encountered the inhospitable man-eating Kyklops Polyphemos, son of Poseidon. He trapped them in his cave, which he sealed by placing an enor-

3

1.Odysseus, bound to the mast of his ship, resists the seductive song of the Sirens. (Stamnos, c. 475-460 BC. British Museum E 440.)

mous rock at the entrance, and then seized two of the men and swallowed them. Odysseus realised that they would only escape through some trick, and put a cunning plan into practice. First he offered the Kyklops wine to drink, and when he was drunk and fell asleep, he heated the trunk of an olive tree in the fire and thrust it powerfully into his opponent's only eye. The following morning, the Kyklops, enraged at what had happened to him, stood outside his cave and felt the backs of his animals as they came out of the cave to go to their grazing ground, intending to catch the men who had blinded him. Odysseus and his comrades, however, had tied themselves underneath the bellies of the sheep, and managed to escape

1

safely to their ships. When Polyphemos realised that the strangers had eluded him, he laid a curse on their leader, that he should lose all his companions, should wander for many years, and when he finally arrived home, would find great misfortune. Polyphemos called upon Poseidon to fulfil his curses and the god, out of sympathy for his offspring, compelled Odysseus to wander the sea for ten years.

When Odysseus came to Aiolia, he was entertained by Aiolos, the lord of the winds; to help Odysseus, Aiolos gave him a flask in which he had shut up all the winds except the one that would take him back to Ithake. During the voyage, however, Odysseus fell asleep and his companions, out of curiosity, opened the flask and set free the winds, who took them back to Aiolia. From there they had to continue their journey unaided, because Aiolos refused to oppose the will of Poseidon for a second time.

The next adventure took place in the land of the Laistrygonians. The inhabitants of this country were enormous, very strong and naturally aggressive. They attacked Odysseus's companions, whom they decimated. The hero managed to escape and save himself together with just a few of them. They next anchored at Aiaia, the island of the goddess Kirke, and sent

2

twenty men to reconnoitre. All of them except Eurylochos, went to the palace of the goddess, who was at first friendly and hospitable; as soon as she had gained their confidence, however, she raised a magic wand and turned them all into swine. When Eurylochos returned in panic to the ship and told the others what had happened, Odysseus decided to get to the bottom of the mystery himself. At this point the gods managed to escape Poseidon's watchful eye for a short time and help the hero. Hermes left

2. Odysseus listens enchanted to the music of a Siren. (Lekythos, 6th c. BC. Athens, National Archaeological Museum 1130.)

Olympos and met Odysseus to give him a plant called *moly*, which would protect him from Kirke's spells. The goddess tried to turn him into a pig, but soon realised that it was useless and in the end, enchanted by his power, she invited him to sleep with her. Before he accepted, however, Odysseus made her swear that she would not harm him and that she would release the spell on his comrades. Odysseus stayed on Kirke's island for a whole year, and shared her bed, but it was always his aim to return to Ithake. The goddess, respecting his wishes, urged him first to go to the Underworld to seek the advice of the prophet Teiresias, and she gave him directions for this difficult and dangerous journey. Odysseus headed north and, following the stream of Ocean, came to the river Acheron and the entrance to the dark kingdom of Hades. There he dug a trench and sacrificed a black ram and a black ewe in honour of Pluto and Persephone. As the blood flowed from the sacrificial victims, thirsty souls gathered around. The first to approach was the soul of Elpenor, an unfortunate companion of Odysseus who had been killed by an accident on the island of Kirke and had remained unburied. He now came to ask for burial and Odysseus promised him that as soon as he returned he would carry out his wishes. When Teiresias appeared, he first slaked his thirst with the blood of the sacrifice and then advised the hero not to allow his comrades to touch the flocks of

Helios when they came to Thrinakia (in Sicily). He also warned him that other misfortunes would be awaiting him in Ithake and that he would have to propitiate Poseidon in the following way: he should take an oar on his shoulder and set out to find the country whose inhabitants did not know what the sea and ships were; when he got there he should stick the oar in the ground and sacrifice a boar, a ram and a bull in honour of the god; then when he returned to Ithake he should offer sacrifices to the twelve gods. Finally, the wise prophet, having predicted that death would come to the hero from the sea, departed. After this Odysseus immediately permitted all the other souls to drink the sacrificial blood, and met with many that he knew and loved.

Homer gives a particularly moving account of his meeting with his mother, Antikleia, who had died of her grief and worry as she waited for him to return. Odysseus also met many of the heroes, including Achilles and Patroklos, Agamemnon, who told him about his own tragic death, and Theseus and Peirithoos, and he saw Minos and Rhadamanthys judging the souls and Sisyphos and Tantalos suffering their eternal punishments.

When he returned to the island of Kirke, he attended to Elpenor's burial and prepared to depart. The goddess warned

him that he would pass by the Sirens, who had women's heads and the bodies of birds, and who enchanted passers-by with their intoxicating singing, making them forget their homelands to stay with them. When Odysseus's ship neared the island of the Sirens, the hero ordered his companions to tie him to the mast and block up their ears with wax. Odysseus was enchanted by the sweet voices of the Sirens, but could not escape from his bonds.

Next the hero had to steer a course between two rocks which were inhabited by two menacing monsters. On one side lived Skylla, a terrible beast with six heads, who snatched anyone that dared to come near and tore them apart, while on the other was Charybdis, who swallowed the sea and then vomited it out creating sudden storms and whirlpools. Odysseus managed to overcome this obstacle, though he lost another six of his companions.

The next port of call was Thrinikia where, heeding the advice of Teiresias, he forbade anyone to touch the flocks of Helios. However, by mischance, bad weather broke out and they were obliged to stay on the island for a month, so that the supplies given to them by Kirke ran out. At one point, when Odysseus was away, Eurylochos was driven by his hunger to persuade the rest to kill some of the

Skylla on the waves, (Bronze sheet, late 4th. c. BC. Athens, National Archeological Museum.)

1. Penelope sits in sorrow next to her loom, and her son, Telemachos stands before her. (Drawing from a skyphos, c. 440 BC. Chiusi, Museo Civico 1831.)

2. Penelope. (Marble statue by Leonidas Drosis. Athens, National Historical Museum.)

animals and then propitiate the god by sacrifices and honours. Helios, however, was slighted and punished them severely: before they could sail away he overturned their ship, sparing only the life of Odysseus. The hero wandered the sea clutching to the ruins of the ship until, after nine days, he came to Ogygia, the island of Kalypso.

Odysseus spent about five years with the beautiful Nymph, who promised him that if he would stay forever with her, she would grant him immortality and eternal youth. He, however, desperately wanted to return to his homeland, and wept as he gazed out to sea and thought of Ithake. When Athena saw her protege in this state, she took pity on him and, taking advantage of Poseidon's absence,

asked Zeus for help. It was at once decided that Hermes should be sent to Kalypso to tell her that it was the order of the gods that she should set Odysseus free, and Athena herself went to Ithake to urge Telemachos to visit Pylos and Sparta in search of news of his father.

Kalypso obeyed the orders of the gods and bade farewell to Odysseus, first helping him to make a raft and supplying him with the necessary provisions. The adventures of the hero were not yet over, however. As Poseidon was returning to Mount Olympos, he noticed the raft and in his anger caused a fearful storm. Odysseus fought with the waves unaided for two days, until he came to the shore of the island of the Phaiacians.

The Phaiacians dwelt on

Scheria and were a highly privileged people: their trees produced fruit at all seasons of the year, and their ships were magic, because they could sail without the aid of captains. Scheria was ruled by Alkinoos and Arete, his wife, who had four sons and a daughter called Nausikaa. On the day that the storm cast up Odysseus on the island, the girl and her friends had gone down to the beach to wash. There she met the hero, who was naked and in distress, took pity on him, and gave him clean clothes, before taking him to her father's palace. Alkinoos readily entertained the stranger, and when he discovered who he was, honoured him with valuable presents and promised that would help him to return to his own land.

And Odysseus indeed came back to Ithake on one of the magic ships of the Phaiacians. The hero was welcomed to the home he had yearned for by Athena, who told him all that had happened during his absence. During the ten years of his wanderings, all trace of him had been lost and many thought that he was dead. The

suitors of his wife Penelope, had established themselves in the palace. One hundred and eight men were eating and drinking daily at the expense of his estate, waiting for Penelope to decide which one she would choose to become her husband. She, however, secretly hoped that Odysseus was still alive, and delayed answering. Meanwhile, the suitors had lost their patience and, to put Penelope in an even more difficult position, were plotting to

2

1

kill her son, Telemachos, when he returned from Sparta, where he had gone to seek news of his father.

These were the difficulties encountered by Odysseus when he returned to Ithake, but he overcame them with the aid of Athena. First of all, the goddess told him to dress as a beggar so that his enemies would not recognise him, and brought Telemachos to him, to protect him from the suitors' conspiracy. When father and son recognised each other, they agreed to work together to restore order to their land.

Odysseus appeared at the palace dressed as a beggar and no-one recognised him apart from his aged dog, Argos, who died as soon as he saw his master. The suitors treated the poor stranger with great contempt,

and he suffered their jeers and attacks. That evening, having advised his son to remove the spears from the walls of the banquet room, he visited Penelope, though he chose not to reveal himself to her yet. He told her that he had heard that her husband was on the island of the Phaiacians, where he had gone to acquire more wealth before returning finally to his home. Although she found it difficult to believe that Odysseus would return to her, Penelope took care of the stranger and asked Eurykleia to wash his feet. Eurykleia, the aged nurse of the hero, recognised him from a mark on his foot, but promised him not to reveal his secret.

Next day, events moved rapidly. Penelope showed the suitors Odysseus's bow and told them that she would marry anyone who could bend it and fire an arrow through twelve axes. One by one the suitors attempted to bend the bow and string an arrow on it, but no-one had the strength. Then Odysseus, still dressed as a beggar, humbly sought permission to try. Everyone laughed at him, but in the end gave permission. Great was their surprise, when the hero succeeded in bending the bow and shooting the arrow through the axes. Odysseus immediately revealed his identity and the suitors tried to escape in panic; they were trapped, however, because Telemachos had closed all the exits, and Odysseus used his bow to take revenge on all those who for ten long years had taken advantage of his palace and his estate.

Only after he had discharged his duty did the hero present himself to his wife in his real form. Penelope tested him to confirm that he was telling the truth, and then welcomed her husband with great emotion. The aged Laertes, the father of Odysseus was equally overjoyed when he saw his son. Odysseus told them all about his adventures, and lived with them happily. He did not fail to propitiate Poseidon, following Teiresias's advice, and died on Ithake many years later, precisely as the prophet had predicted: when Telegonos, his son by Kirke, arrived at the island in his ships, he clashed with the locals and killed their king, not knowing who he was.

2

2. Bust of Homer. (Roman copy. Boston, Museum of Fine Arts.)

3. Odysseus meets his wife, Penelope. (Relief from Milos, c. 475-450 BC. Louvre CA 105.)

3

OEDIPUS
AND THE THEBAN CYCLE

1. Oedipus meets
the Sphinx before
the elders of
Thebes.
(Pelike, c. 460
BC. Vienna, Kun-
st Historisches
Museum IV
3728.)

THE EARLY YEARS OF
OEDIPUS' LIFE

Aeschylus told the dramatic story of Oedipus and his family in the trilogy formed by the tragedies *Laios*, *Oedipus*, and *Seven Against Thebes*, and the

1

satyr play *Sphinx*. Only the third of these survives, but the plot of the others may be restored on the basis of other tragedies inspired by the same myth.

The story begins when Laios succeeded his father Labdakos, the son of Polydoros, to the throne of Thebes. The young king, and his wife Iokaste ruled happily over the glorious land founded by their great-grandfather, Kadmos. The years passed and because the couple had no children, they decided to consult the Delphic oracle. The oracle warned them that Thebes would be preserved only if they remained childless; otherwise it was ordained that the father would be killed by the hand of his son. Ignoring the prophetic words of Apollo, Iokaste became pregnant and brought a male child into the world. In their panic, the two parents attempted to cheat destiny: they ordered a faithful servant to abandon the new-born child on Mount Kithairon. The king even bound the young boy's legs together with chains around his ankle, to prevent him escaping. The servant, however, took pity on the baby and saved his life by giving him to a Corinthian shepherd he met on the mountain. The shepherd took the child back to his own land and delivered him to the king and queen of Corinth, Polybos and Merope, who were childless and received the child joyfully, calling him Oedipus, because his feet were swollen from the chains.

Oedipus was brought up as a prince in Corinth with the prospect of inheriting the throne of his father, without, of course, being aware of his true identity. The misfortunes began when someone accused him of not being the real son of the king. Distressed, Oedipus set out for the Delphic oracle in order to learn the truth. The Pythia, however, did not give a straight answer to the hero's question, but simply told him that it was ordained that he would kill his father and marry his mother. Shaken by the words of the oracle, Oedipus decided never to return to Corinth and began to wander from place to place. His travels gradually led him to the fateful meeting with his real father. In one of the narrow passes in Phokis, Oedipus's path crossed with that of Laios, who was travelling to Delphi to ask the oracle what had been the fate of the child he had abandoned on Mount Kithairon. The proud youth refused to give way to allow the king to pass, the two men clashed, and Oedipus killed Laios; the first part of the oracle had been fulfilled. The unhappy youth continued his wanderings unsuspecting, while

2. The statue of the Sphinx which was dedicated by the Naxians in the sanctuary of Apollo at Delphi. (c. 570-560 BC. Delphi Museum.)

2

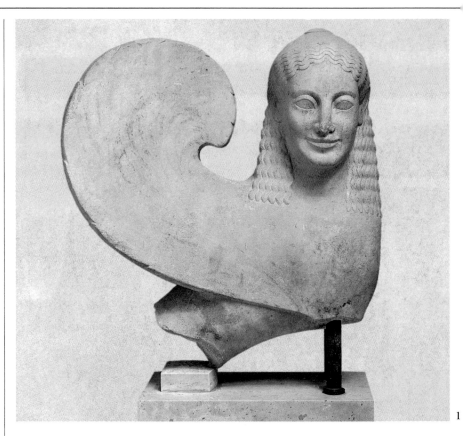

Marble statue of a sphinx. (540 - 530 π.Χ. Acropolis Museum).

his dead father's attendants returned to Thebes with the bad news.

Kreon, the brother of queen Iokaste, was appointed successor to Laios and ruled the land together with the venerable elders.

THE RIDDLE OF THE SPHINX

At this time the diabolical Sphinx, a terrible monster with a woman's head and the body of a winged lion, appeared in Thebes and proclaimed that she would stop wreaking havoc in the land and destroying its inhabitants only if someone could solve the following riddle: 'What being may have two feet, four feet, or three feet, is the only one of all the beings that move on earth, in the air, and in the sea, that can change its form, and moves more slowly when it has most feet'. The Sphinx asked this riddle of anyone who went near her, and killed those who gave the wrong answer. In his despair, Kreon proclaimed throughout the whole of Greece, that anyone who succeeded in ridding Thebes of this suffering would become king of the land and would marry Iokaste. This proclamation brought Oedipus back to his birthplace. When the Sphinx encountered Oedipus she asked the riddle. The hero gave the correct answer, that the riddle referred to man, and in her rage, the Sphinx jumped from the rocks of the acropolis of Thebes and was killed. Thebes had been saved, and the 'saviour' married the queen, unaware of the tragic nature of his deeds.

THE REIGN OF OEDIPUS

Oedipus and Iokaste ruled at Thebes for several years and had four children: Eteokles, Polyneikes, Ismene, and Antigone. Circumstances, however, led the king to realise his real identity (Sophocles, *Oedipus Tyrannus*). The cause was a drought that broke out at Thebes causing the death of many of its citizens. Oedipus, anxious for the fate of his country, sent Kreon to Delphi to ask how they could be rid of this scourge, and the god advised them to purify themselves of the pollution of the murder of Laios by driving the murderer from the city. The words of the oracle shocked Oedipus, who immediately proclaimed, with promises and imprecations, that he was determined to do everything he could to find the murderer, unaware, of course, that he himself was responsible for Laios's death. He first summoned the prophet Teiresias and made him reveal the truth.

When the prophet broke his silence and revealed the tragic events, the king refused to believe him.

As the shocking truth began to be revealed, Oedipus recalled his clash in the past in Phokis, and his fears were confirmed when one of Laios's servants, the only one who had survived the conflict, recognised the king. His testimony was irrefutable, because he was the same servant who had taken the new-born child to abandon it on Mount Kithairon.

The royal couple met with a dramatic end. Iokaste hanged herself and Oedipus pierced his eyes with the pins that adorned the dress worn by his dead mother and wife. The hero blinded himself to conceal his unutterable shame in darkness.

The cloak of silence that had apparently protected Oedipus, was now lifted forever, marking the beginning of the end for the kingdom of Thebes. The blind king fled the land accompanied by his daughter, Antigone.

2. Corinthian aryballos. 7th c. BC (Delphi Museum.)

2

253

THE SEVEN
AGAINST THEBES

The throne of Oedipus passed to his two sons, but they were unable to share power peacefully. After many fruitless negotiations, Eteokles became king and Polyneikes fled the city discontented, his only inheritance being the wedding presents of Harmonia, the wife of Kadmos.

The exiled brother went to Argos, arriving in he city the same night as Tydeus, the son of Oineus and Periboia, who had similarly been driven out of Kalydon to seek purification for the murder of one of his relatives. When the two youths met in the courtyard in front of Adrastos's palace, they quarrelled and came to blows. The king was awakened by their voices, but seeing them wrestling like wild animals, he realised that this was the fulfilment of a prophecy by the oracle that had told him to take the boar and the lion as his sons-in-law. He immediately intervened to separate the rivals, assuring them that they were both welcome in his palace. The relationship between Polyneikes and Tydeus developed into a strong friendship, and also kinship, for they married the two daughters of Adrastos, the former Argeia and the latter Deipyle. Adrastos offered his sons-in-law a life of ease and recognised them as his official heirs.

The two youths, however, had ambitions of returning to their own countries to claim the rights of which they had been deprived by exile. Adrastos, who effectively had no other choice, agreed to help them by sending his forces first against Thebes and then against Kalydon. Before they set forth, they made one last attempt to settle the matter peacefully. Eteokles, however, refused to negotiate, even though Tydeus went to Thebes with peaceful intentions. Back in Argos, preparations began for the expedition, with the aim of assembling forces from neighbouring cities.

Adrastos at once turned to his brother-in-law, Amphiaraos. In the past these two men had quarrelled about affairs of state, but when they finally settled their differences, they sealed the reconciliation by a marriage between Amphiaraos and Eriphyle, Adrastos's sister, swearing an oath that in the future she would resolve any differences between them. Amphiaraos, who in addition to being a competent general was also a healer and a gifted prophet, foresaw the calamitous end of this expedition and refused to take part. Adrastos, however, knowing that he would make a very valuable contribution, refused to accept Amphiaraos's decision, and the two called upon Eriphyle to resolve their dispute. She had been bribed, however, by Polyneikes, with the necklace of Harmonia (the precious wedding present given by Aphrodite to her daughter) and therefore took

her brother's side, betraying her husband. Adrastos could not foreswear his oath and therefore had to accept his wife's decision. Before setting forth, however, he handed his sword to his son, Alkmaion, ordering him to avenge his death by punishing his mother and undertaking an expedition against the Thebans.

When the preparations were completed, the army of the Argives and their allies set off for Thebes, but Polyneikes first went to Athens to find his father. After blinding himself, Oedipus had fled to Athens with Antigone (Sophocles, *Oedipus in Kolonos*). In the suburb of Kolonos, he had fallen as a suppliant at the altar of the Eumenides, and, having told his story to the venerable Athenian elders, had asked them to summon the ruler of the country, which at this time was Theseus, so that he could ask him to be allowed to die in Attica. While Oedipus was awaiting for Theseus, Ismene, his other daughter, came to Kolonos, to tell him about the war that had broken out between her brothers and to warn him that both of them would attempt to win him over, because according to the Delphic oracle, the battle would be won by the one that had Oedipus on his side. The first to arrive in Athens was Kreon, acting as the emissary of Eteokles, who tried to blackmail Oedipus into cooperating by arresting his daughters. Theseus intervened,

Amphiaraos entrusts his sword to his son, Alkmaion (Drawing of a beu krater, c. 440 BC. Syracuse Museum 18421.)

however, and drove him from the land. The next to arrive was Polyneikes, who attempted to win over his father by his moving words. Oedipus, however, was annoyed at the behaviour of his children and their thirst for power, and in his anger he uttered a curse that each would be killed by the hand of the other. Immediately after this the unfortunate king, after receiving a message from the gods in the form of a thunderbolt from Zeus, went off to meet Charon, who would take him to the Underworld. Theseus went ahead of the blind old man and promised him that he would offer help and protection to his daughters.

The clash between the Argives and the Thebans was to lead to the tragic end of Eteokles and Polyneikes, (Aeschylus, *Seven Against Thebes*). Eteokles was told about the arrival of the enemy while he was attempting to reassure the Theban women, who in panic had sought asylum at the altars of the gods. Each of the seven Argive generals had drawn up his forces in front of the seven gates in the walls of Thebes, in the following order: Tydeus, Kapaneus, Eteoklos, Hippomedon, Parthenopaios, Amphiaraos and Polyneikes. Eteokles gave his final orders to his army and decided to defend the seventh gate himself, fighting against his brother. The first step towards the fulfilment of their father's curse had been taken, and the battle ended in the retreat of the Argives, and with the two brothers killing each other.

This tragic event was not the end of the misfortunes of the family of Oedipus, however. Kreon, who came to power in Thebes once more, buried Eteokles with great honours, but forbade the burial of Polyneikes and refused to hand over the bodies of the seven generals to the Argives. This injustice and impiety towards the dead aroused a hostile reaction on the part of many. Foremost amongst them was Antigone, who declared categorically that she would not allow her brother to remain unburied.

Kreon decided to place a guard around Polyneikes's body, so that the dead man should remain exposed and be eaten by the animals, which caused the situation to deteriorate (Sophocles, *Antigone*). Incensed at this act of barbarism, Antigone attempted symbolically to throw a little earth on the abandoned body of her beloved brother, for which she was arrested, led to the king and finally punished by imprisonment. Kreon refused to revoke his order, even though he knew that as long as the established burial customs did not take place, the soul of the dead man would not find serenity, but was condemned to eternal torment. It was only when the prophet Teiresias warned him that an act of such great impiety directly endangered his life that he was obliged to allow Polyneikes to be buried. Kreon did not go unpunished, however. He first lost his son, Haimon, who committed suicide when he learned that Antigone, his fiance, had hanged herself in prison, and then his wife, Eurydike, who could not bear the pain of the death of her child.

Kreon's decision not to hand over the bodies of the seven generals to the Argives had equally dramatic consequences. The mothers of the dead men decided to seek the aid of Theseus, who was king of Athens at this time (Euripides, *Iketides*). Accompanied by Adrastos, the only general to survive the expedition, they came to Attica. The women feli as suppliants at the altar of the goddess Demeter at Eleusis, asking Aithra to persuade her son to help them. Theseus listened carefully to his mother, and then spoke respectfully of the dead and compassionately of their relatives, and agreed to satisfy the women's demand. To this end he led an expedition against Thebes. The Thebans, who were

Amphiaraos heals a sick man. (Votive relief, c. 400-370 AD. Athens, National Archaeological Museum 3369.)

257

already weakened by the war, succumbed quickly to the Athenian forces and were obliged to hand over the bodies of the Argive generals. The bodies were taken Eleusis, where they were buried with the appropriate honours by their wives and children.

The conflict was not yet at an end, however. Before departing for Thebes, Amphiaraos had given his son, Alkmaion, his sword, foreseeing that he himself would not return from the war. And indeed, as he was racing in his chariot to escape the enemy, the earth opened and swallowed him. This event was interpreted as a divine sign, and the first sanctuary of Amphiaraos was built on this spot: ever since then, Amphiaraos has been worshipped as a prophet and a healer-god.

THE EXPEDITION OF THE EPIGONI

Another expedition against Thebes was organised by Alkmaion, who had sworn to avenge his father's death, and Thersandros, the son of Polyneikes, who wanted to lay claim to the throne of Thebes. The armies of the Epigoni assembled at Argos ten years after the first conflict. Their leaders were: Alkmaion, son of Amphiaraos, Thersandros, son of Polyneikes, Diomedes, son of Tydeus, Sthenelos, son of Kapaneus, Promachos, son of Parthenopaios, Medon, son of Eteoklos, and Polydoros, son of Hippomedon. The aged Adrastos offered useful advice and instructions to the young generals and sent his son, Aigialaeus with them.

Thebes was ruled by Laodamas, son of Eteokles, who undertook the defence of his country. When the Argive forces reached Boeotia, the Thebans began to attack, striking at the camp of their rivals. The first to be killed was Aigialaeus, but the Epigoni swiftly regrouped their forces and then Alkmaion fatally wounded Laodamas. The Thebans retreated within their walls, panic-stricken at the death of their king. The Argives then attacked and were victorious. The kingdom of Kadmos had been completely destroyed — so comprehensively that it is not mentioned by Homer in the list of the Greek forces that took part in the expedition against Troy.

1-2. The seven Argive generals prepare for the expedition against Thebes. (Kylix, c. 490-480 BC. Louvre G 271).

2

PERSEUS

THE EARLY YEARS OF PERSEUS' LIFE

Perseus came from the Argolid and was the son of Zeus and Danae. Before turning to the adventures, we may briefly examine his family tree, starting with his ancestor, Belos, who ruled in Africa. Belos was succeeded by his sons, who divided his kingdom: Danaos ruled in Libya with his wife, Europa (who shared the same name as the daughter of Agenor) and his fifty daughters, and Aigyptos in Arabia with Euryrrhoe and their fifty sons. The two brothers soon clashed over matters of state, however, and to protect his daughters, Danaos left his birthplace and came to Argos, the land of his distant forebear Io. Aigyptos, however, had greater ambitions. After some years he appeared at Argos and on the pretext of being reconciled with Danaos sought to marry his sons to his brother's daughters. Danaos was compelled to agree, but avenged himself on Aigyptos by a trick, advising his daughters to kill their husbands on the first night of the marriage. Only Hypermnestra failed to obey her father, out of love for her husband, Lynkeus, by whom she had a son, Abas. The children

1. Danae with the baby Perseus in the box. (Fragment of a krater, c. 450 BC. Elis, Archaeological Collection.)

1

of Abas were two famous kings of the Argolid, Akrisios, who ruled at Argos, and Proitos, king of Tiryns (a forebear of Adrastos, who took part in the campaign of the seven generals against Thebes).

Akrisios's daughter, Danae, was the mother of Perseus. The king imprisoned the attractive Danae in an underground dungeon to prevent her from marrying, because an oracle had predicted that he would be killed by his grandson. Zeus, however, was captivated by the girl's beauty and, since nothing could stop his passion, came to Danae in the form of golden rain. Danae brought Perseus into the world and brought him up without her father's knowledge in her dark dungeon, but the baby's crying betrayed her secret. Terrified, Akrisios put both mother and child in a box and threw them into the sea. The waves carried them to Seriphos, into the nets of the fisherman Diktys, who offered them protection and a home.

When Perseus grew up, he went to a banquet in the palace of Polydektes, the king of the island. The proud young man behaved boastfully and arrogantly towards the ruler of the land, who threatened that if he didn't succeed in bringing him the head of Medusa, he would marry Danae against her will. The hero found himself in a difficult position, but had to defend his mother's honour at all costs.

THE BEHEADING OF MEDUSA

Phorkys and Keto, the children of Gaia and Okeanos — two of the oldest gods in the world — gave birth to the famous Gorgons, who were known by the names Sthenno, Euryale and Medusa. The Gorgons were three female monsters with brazen claws, gold wings, boar's tusks,

2. Zeus approaches Danae in the form of golden rain. (Bell krater, c. 430 BC. Athens, National Archaeological Museum 12593.)

2

1

1. Perseus and the Graiai. (Pyxis, c. 400-350 BC. Athens, National Archaeological Museum 1291.)

and snakes instead of hair, who lived remote from the world probably in the far East, near the garden of the Hesperides.

Medusa was the only mortal one of the three sisters and, according to an interesting version of the myth, had once been very beautiful and dwelt in the far North. Wishing to see the sun, which never appeared in her country, she asked Athena for permission to visit the South, but the goddess refused. In her bitterness, Medusa dared to say that Athena had not granted her the favour out of jealousy of her beauty. The goddess was enraged at the girl's conceitedness and punished her by turning the locks of her hair into snakes, cursing her that her gaze would turn to stone anyone who dared to look her in the eyes.

Perseus had to behead this monstrous woman, and Athena and Hermes undertook to assist him. The gods told him that to be successful he would first have to take from the Nymphs a pair of winged sandals, so that he would not tread on the earth, a magic cap which, when he wore it, would make him invisible, and a magic bag to carry the head of the Gorgon. The residence of the Nymphs was known only by the Graiai, three fearful beings who shared one eye and one tooth between them. On his long journey, Perseus first met the Graiai, and blackmailed them by stealing their precious single eye, so managing to get from them the information that he needed. The episode is depicted on the lid of a pyxis in the Athens National Archaeological Museum: the three women are seated, and one of them gives the eye to another, while Perseus comes between them and snatches it from their hands; also present are Athena, Poseidon, Hermes and an aged man, who may be Phorkys, Medusa's father.

After he had visited the Nymphs, the hero went to the far East. He found Medusa asleep, and approached her without treading on the earth and wearing the cap that made him invisible. The problem was that he had to avoid looking her in the eyes so as not to be turned to stone by her gaze.

2

2. The gorgoneion and Pegasus on the shield of Athena. (Drawing from an amphora, c. 490 BC. Basel, Archaeological Museum Ka 418.)

3. The beheaded Medusa has fallen to the ground, while Perseus makes off with her head, with the assistance of Athena. (Hydria, c. 460 BC. British Museum E 181.)

3

With the aid of Athena and using his shield as a mirror he cut off the head of the fearful Gorgon with a sickle that was given to him by Hermes, and put it into his magic bag. When the hero had successfully completed his mission, he gave the head of Medusa to Athena, who had helped him, and she wore it on her aegis in order to turn her enemies to stone with its gaze. The head of the Medusa (known as the gorgoneion) was a very popular motif in ancient Greek art and was rendered in great detail: it is surrounded by snakes, has two huge wide-open eyes, and sticks its tongue out mockingly at the viewer. The gorgoneion probably had an apotropaic significance. Its frequent depiction in the sculpture and vase-painting of the Archaic (7th-6th c. BC) and Classical (5th c. BC) period is possibly due to the belief that its magical powers and terrible appearance were able to avert the forces of evil.

1. Perseus has just beheaded the Medusa. He holds her head and stands on the body of the dead Gorgon. The hero lowers the head to the ground in order to avoid the deadly gaze of his foe. (Bronze statue, by Benvenuto Cellini, 1500-1571. Florence.)

THE TRIUMPH OF PERSEUS

Perseus returned in triumph to Seriphos and proudly showed the head of Medusa to Polydektes, who was immediately turned to stone when he looked at it. The hero made Diktys king of the island and set off for the Argolid, with the aim of persuading his grandfather that he had no intention of killing him. He found Proitos ruling in Argos, however, and learned that Akrisios was in exile in Larisa. After punishing Proitos by showing him the head of the Gorgon, Perseus went to meet his grandfather, desiring to be reconciled with him. The event was celebrated by athletic contests, though these had a tragic end: as Perseus was throwing the discus, he missed his aim and fatally struck Akrisios. It had been demonstrated once again that divine oracles are always fulfilled, and that human will is not capable of averting destiny.

The hero returned to the Argolid to claim the throne that he had inherited. He gave the kingdom of Argos, however to Megapenthes, son of Proitos, and in return took the kingdom of Tiryns.

Perseus ruled at Tiryns and later also incorporated Mycenae in his kingdom. He married Andromeda, the daughter of Kepheus, king of Ethiopia, whom he had saved from a menacing sea monster, as he returned from the

2

land of the Gorgons. From this marriage were born four sons and one daughter: Elektryon, Alkaios, Perses and Thenelos, and Gorgophone. Elektryon was the father of Alkmene who gave birth to Herakles, and Alkaios was the father of her husband, Amphitryon. According to Aeschylus, Perses was the founder of the Persian race. Sthenelos married Nikippe, the daughter of Pelops and Hippodameia, and became the father of Eurystheus, whom Herakles served when he carried out his twelve labours. Finally, Gorgophone was the mother of Tyndareus, king of Sparta and father of Klytaimnestra and Helen, who bound the fortunes of his family to those of the Atreidai marrying his daughters to Menelaos and Agamemnon.

2. Perseus beheads the Medusa, with Athena next to him. (Metope from temple C. at Selinos, c. 540 BC. Palermo, National Museum.)

PEGASUS AND BELLEROPHON

From the neck of the beheaded Medusa sprang Pegasus and Chrysaor, the offspring of Poseidon, who had slept with her, probably when she was still beautiful. Chrysaor was father of the triple-bodied Geryones, one of the opponents of Herakles. Pegasus was a powerful winged horse, which the god gave to another of his sons, Bellerophon.

Bellerophon lived in Corinth, with Pegasus. He was the grandson of Sisyphos, the only mortal who had successfully cheated death twice, and his mother was Eurynome. On one of his journeys Bellerophon visited Tiryns and was entertained in the palace of Proitos. The problems began when the king's wife, Stheneboia, fell in love with the young visitor and tried to win him. Bellerophon, respecting his host, did not respond to her invitations, but Stheneboia took her revenge by accusing him of having attempted to seduce her. Proitos be-

1. The Gorgon. (Gold sheet from the decoration of a gold and ivory statue, 6th c. BC. Delphi Museum.)

2. Medusa with her children Pegasus and Chrysaor. (From the west pediment of the temple of Artemis on Corfu, c. 580 BC. Corfu, Archaeological Museum.)

1

lieved his wife's words and punished Bellerophon by sending
him to serve his father-in-law
Iobates, the king of Lykia.

Iobates, in response to the request of his son-in-law, assigned
impossible tasks to the hero with
the aim of causing his death.
One of these was to exterminate
the Chimaira, a destructive
monster that belched fire from
its mouth, and had the body of a
lion, the tail of a snake, and the
head of a goat on its back. Bellerophon, riding on Pegasus, succeeded in killing the Chimaira
by striking it with his spear. The
hero also successfully carried
out the other labours assigned
to him and thus won the favour
of Iobates, who in the end re-

3. Bellerophon, riding on Pegasus, kills
   the Chimaira with his spear.
   (Pelike, c. 430 BC, Louvre G 535.)

3

1. Bellerophon and the Chimaira.
(Mosaic from Parundorf, 3rd c. AD. Austria, Eisenstadt Landesmusum.)

2

tained him and made him his son-in-law.

After all these successes, however, Bellerophon became very boastful and believed that he could reach the gods. He mounted on Pegasus and began to rise higher and higher in the heaven. The divine horse, however, threw him from its back and he fell humbled to earth. Bellerophon continued his life wandering from place to place and avoiding gods and men. Pegasus ascended to Mount Olympos to serve Eos, who brought the dawn at the beginning of each day.

2. Two Pegasi in bust. (Bronze sheet from male jewellery, c. 575 BC. Herakleion Museum 3006.)

3

3. Bellerophon and the Chimaira. (Epinetron, c. 430 BC. Athens, National Archaeological Museum 3179.)

PHRIXOS AND HELLE

1. Phrixos travels to Kolchis on the golden ram. (Terracotta relief from Milos, c. 470 BC. Athens, National Archaeological Museum 4196.)

Phrixos and Helle were descended from Thessaly, but grew up in Boeotia. Their father, Athamas, the brother of Kretheus, the king of Iolkos, slept with their mother, the goddess Nephele, while he was still living in his fatherland.

Later, however, Athamas rejected the love of the goddess in order to marry Kadmos's daughter Ino. Having abandoned Nephele, he settled with his children in the kingdom of his father-in-law in Thebes. Phrixos and Helle grew up there with Learchos and Melikertes, the two sons of Athamas by his second wife.

Ino, however, never loved Nephele's children and decided to kill them so that her own sons

1

2

2. Ino chases Phrixos, while he departs on the ram sent to him by his mother, Nephele. (Drawing from an amphora, c. 430 BC. Naples, Museo Nazionale Archeologico 2335.)

would be her husband's only successors. To achieve her aim, she devised a cunning scheme: first she persuaded her husband's subjects to complain that the country was threatened by drought, and then bribed the emissaries sent to the Delphic oracle to declare to the king that according to the god, only the sacrifice of Phrixos would save the land. Athamas had no other choice. When everything was ready for the sacrifice, however, Nephele intervened and prevented Ino's plan from being carried out. The goddess sent Hermes's ram with the golden fleece, which took Phrixos and Helle on its back and carried them high into the heavens.

Fleeing far from Greece, Nephele's two children were safe. As they travelled above the modern straights of the Dardanelles, however, Helle slipped from the animal's back and fell into the sea, which has since that time been called the Hellespont. Phrixos continued his journey alone to the far East, until the sacred ram finally brought him to Kolchis. This land was ruled by one of the sons of Helios, Aietes, who had two daughters, Chalkiope and Medea. Aietes welcomed Phrixos to his palace and readily entertained him. The hero soon won the trust of the king and married Chalkiope.

Phrixos lived the rest of his life in Kolchis. He sacrificed the ram that had saved his life, in honour of Zeus and gave its precious fleece to his father-in-law. He also placed the golden fleece in the sacred grove of Ares and set a terrible serpent to guard it. Nobody had dared to draw near and provoke the menacing beast until Jason came to Kolchis (see pp. 224-227).

GENEALOGICAL TREE

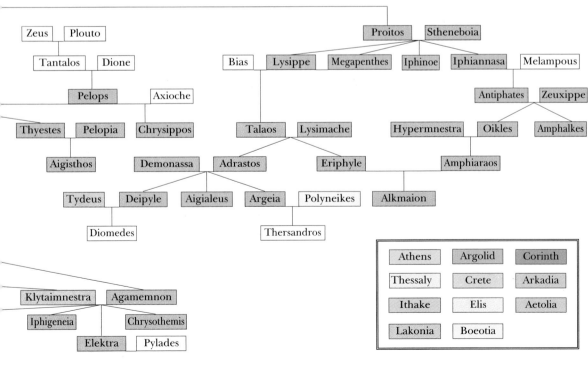

EPILOGUE

1. Bronze theatre mask. (4th c. BC. Athens, National Archaeological Museum.)

Myths played a very important role in Ancient Greek societies, because they were directly connected with their history and religion. Myths were woven to explain the natural phenomena that affected the daily lives of men, and also to narrate the historical events that marked the evolution of civilisation. Mythology was enriched throughout the whole of antiquity, with every place creating its own myths or producing variants of earlier ones, according to its own experience and needs.

Through art and the written sources, we now know a great number of these myths, and are called upon to understand and interpret the role they played in the societies that created them. This is a difficult, never-ending task, which, as we have seen, produces conclusions that are mere hypotheses, since we can never fully enter into the ancient Greek mentality and tradition. Modern research is based mainly on analysis of the motifs of which the myths are composed, and seeks to interpret these in the light of their social and historical context. Many of the motifs in Greek mythology are repeated with different leading actors. Perhaps the most popular of them is the family conflict revolving around power. The first to become embroiled in this kind of clash were the earliest gods, who did not succeed each other peacefully: Kronos usurped the power of Ouranos, to be defeated in his turn by his son, Zeus. In the same way, Zeus prevented the birth of the son that would have been given him by Metis, when he learned that this child would surpass him strength. In the world of mortals, this kind of conflict arose mainly between brothers: we may recall by way of example Atreus and Thyestes, Aigyptos and Danaos, Proitos and Akrisios, and Eteokles and Polyneikes. These and other similar tales involving the deeds of men and heros, probably reflect human ambitions and dreams.

Only the gods are all-powerful, however, and can fulfil all their desires by using every possible means. They frequently transform themselves or transform their victims in order to achieve their ends: Zeus assumes the form of a bull to abduct Europa and Hera punishes Io by turning her into a cow. The most precious gift they have to offer their favourites is immortality: it was for this purpose that Thetis baptised the new-born Achilles in the fire, as Demeter also did with the young Demophon. Fire is transformed into myth not only because it evoked awe in man, as indeed did the other elements of nature, but also because its contribution to the evolution of civilisation became apparent from a very early date. The possession of so important a tool and weapon naturally demanded an act of daring on the scale of that of Prometheus.

Many heroes were not merely the favourites of the gods but their offspring. The relationship between a god and a mortal woman, and vice versa, is a very common motif in Greek mythology. Herakles and Perseus, two of the sons of Zeus, and Theseus, the son of Poseidon, owe their superhuman strength to their divine descent. These heroes are called upon to face powerful foes, such as remorseless robbers and murderers, and also deadly beasts that threaten the social entity. They finally triumph thanks to their strength and the assistance of the gods, and tradition glorifies them by singing their adventures. The myths that tell of their feats form a model of courage and nobility, and their fight against various fantastic beings therefore symbolises man's struggle against unknown, and therefore terrifying, natural phenomena.

Every hero has his own story

2. A maenad reclines on a panther skin. (Marble statue, 117-138 AD. Athens, National Archaeological Museum 261.)

2

275

and his own personal labours, but there are also several cases in which many powerful men work together to confront an enemy or to carry out a mission. The choicest young men from the whole of Greece took part in the Argonaut expedition and the hunt for the Kalydonian boar, and when Herakles set out on his expedition against the Amazons and after that against Troy, he took with him warriors who were his equal, such as Theseus. And the most important kings of Greece took part in the famous Trojan War with their armies. All these myths reflect the adventures of the ancient Greeks in the Aegean and the Mediterranean in general, since Greece's geographical position acted as a stimulus to the evolution of shipping in antiquity, both for trade and for reasons of expansion.

The voyages and adventures of Greek sailors belonged to the world of myth and passed into eternity, like all the events that marked the troubled heroic age. It is true that the historical value of myths is debatable, but their contribution to the study of ancient Greek civilisation is invaluable. In the ancient world, men tell their stories through myths, and mythology is therefore an expression of their attempt to embellish and elevate their personal experience of life.

1. Dionysos with his retinue. (Kalyx krater, c. 490 BC. Louvre G 162.)

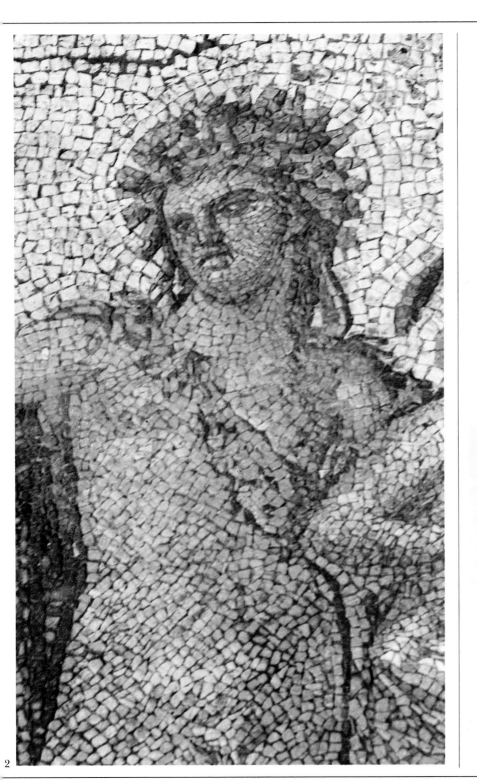

2. Dionysos crosses the sea on a chariot.
(Mosaic from the so-called 'Villa of Dionysos' at Dion, late 2nd c. AD. Dion.)

2

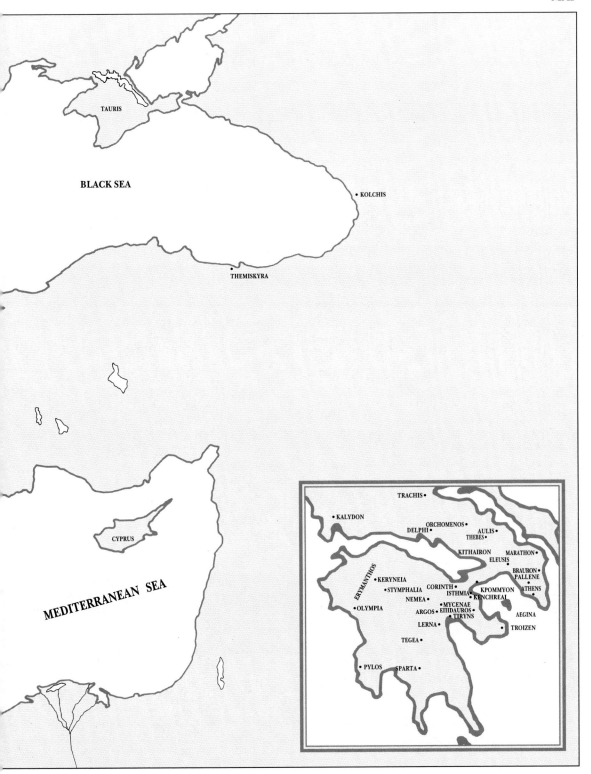

TAURIS

BLACK SEA

• KOLCHIS

• THEMISKYRA

CYPRUS

MEDITERRANEAN SEA

TRACHIS •

• KALYDON

DELPHI • ORCHOMENOS •   AULIS •
                        THEBES •

KITHAIRON   MARATHON •
            ELEUSIS •

ERYMANTHOS   • KERYNEIA   BRAURON •
                                 PALLENE •
• STYMPHALIA   CORINTH •
               ISTHMIA •   KPOMMYON   ATHENS •
NEMEA •   KENCHREAI
• OLYMPIA   • MYCENAE
ARGOS • EΠIDAUROS •   AEGINA
        • TIRYNS
LERNA •
                           • TROIZEN
TEGEA •

• PYLOS   SPARTA •

GENERAL BIBLIOGRAPHY

Armantrout, G. L., *The Seven Against Thebes in Greek Art* (1991).

Bell, R.E., *Dictionary of Classical Mythology* (1982).

Bieber, M., *The History of Greek and Roman Theatre* (1961).

Birchall, A. and Corbett, P.E., *Greek Gods and Heroes* (1974).

Boardman, J., *Athenian Black Figure Vases: A Handbook* (1974).

Boardman, J., *Athenian Red Figure Vases: A Handbook* (1975).

Boardman, J., *The Parthenon and its Sculptures* (1985).

Boardman, J., *Athenian Red Figure Vases, the Classical Period: A Handbook* (1989).

Bothmer, D. Von, *Amazons in Greek Art* (1957).

Bremmer, J. (ed.), ' *What is a Greek Myth?'*, *Interpretations of Greek Mythology* (1987).

Brommer, F., *Theseus: die Taten des griechischen Helden in der antiken Kunst und Literatur* (1982).

Odysseus: die Taten und Leiden des Helden in der antiken Kunst und Literatur (1983).

Heracles: The Twelve Labors of the Hero in Ancient Art and Literature (1985).

Brunel, P. (ed.), *Companion of Literary Myths, Heroes and Archetypes* (1992).

D. Buitron and B. Cohen *et al.*, *The Odyssey and Ancient Art. An Epic in World and Image* (1992).

Burkert, W., *Greek Religion* (1985).

Burkert, W., *Structure and History in Greek Mythology and History* (1979).

Buxton, R., *Imaginary Greece. The Contents of Mythology* (1994).

Carpenter, T.H., *Art and Myth in Ancient Greece. A Handbook* (1991).

Chamay, J., *Mythologie grecque. La guerre de Troie* (1984).

Daltrop, G., *Die Kalydonische Jagd in der Antike* (1966).

Dowden, K., *The Uses of Greek Mythology* (1992).

Edmunds, L. (ed.), *Approaches to Greek Myth* (1990).

Graf, F., *Greek Mythology. An Introduction* (trans. Thomas Marier, 1993).

Grant, M. and Hazel, J., *Who's Who? in Classical Mythology* (1973).

Graves, R., *Greek Myths* (1955).

Grimal, P., *Dictionnaire de la mythologie grecque et romaine* (1991).

Kaempf-Dimitriadou, S., *Die Liebe der Götter in der attischen Kunst des 5. Jhs. v. Chr.*, *Antike Kunst.* (1979).

Kakridis I. Ih., *et al.*, Ελληνική μυθολογία, 1-5 (1986).

Kerenyi, K., Η μυθολογία των Ελλήνων (1974).

Kirk, G.S., *Myth. Its Meaning and Functions in Ancient Greek ad other Cultures* (1970).

Lesky, A., *A History of Greek Literature* (1966).

Lexicon Iconographicum Mythologiae Classicae (1981-).

Metzger, H., *Les représentations dans la céramique attique du IVe siècle (1951).*

Metzger, H., *Recherches sur l'imagerie athénienne* (1965).

Moret, J. M., *Oedipe, la sphinx et les Thébains. Essai de mythologie iconographique* (1984).

Neils, J., *The Youthful deeds of Theseus* (1987).

Nilsson, M., *History of Ancient Greek Religion* (1963).

Papahatzis, N.D., Η θρησκεία στην αρχαία Ελλάδα (1987).

Parke, H.W., *Festivals of the Athenians* (1977).

Schefold, K., *Myth and Legend in Early Greek Art* (1966).

Schefold, K, and Jung, F., *Die Göttersage in der klassischen und hellenistischen Kunst* (1981).

Schefold, K., *Die Urkönige, Perseus, Bellerophon, Herakles und Theseus in der klassischen und hellenistischen Kunst* (1988).

Schefold, K. and Jung, F., *Die Sagen von den Argonauten von Theben und Troia in der klassischen und Hellenistischen Kunst* (1989).

Simon, E., *The Ancient Theatre* (1982).

Simon, E., *Festivals of Attica* (1983).

Stewart, A., *Greek Sculpture. An Exploration* (1990).

Touchefeu-Meynier, O., *Thèmes odysséens dans l'art antique* (1968).

Trendall, A.D and Webster, T.B.L., *Illustrations of Greek Drama* (1971).

Vernant, J.P., and Vidal-Naquet, P., *Myth et Tragidie en Grèce ancienne*, vol. I, II (1972, 1986).

Vernant, J.P., *Myth and Society in Ancient Greece*

(μτφρ. 1983).
Vollkommer, R., *Herakles in the Art of Classical Greece* (1988).

Walker, J.H., *Theseus and Athens* (1995).
Woodford, S., *The Trojan War in Ancient Art* (1993).

INDEX

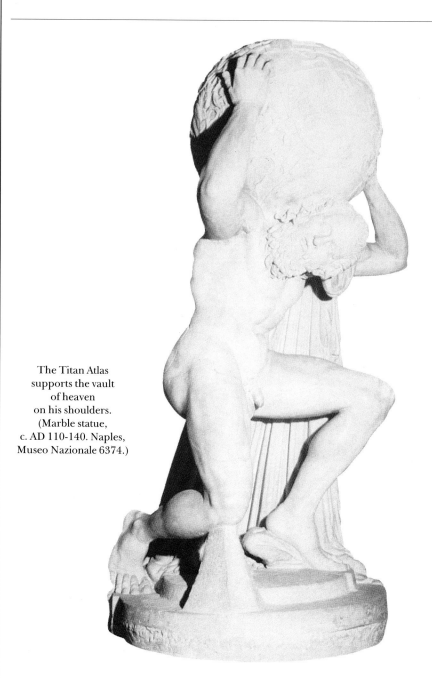

The Titan Atlas
supports the vault
of heaven
on his shoulders.
(Marble statue,
c. AD 110-140. Naples,
Museo Nazionale 6374.)

DESIGN: KOSTAS ADAM
TEXT: MAPILENA CAPABATEA
TRANSLATION : DAVID HARDY
LAY OUT: KPISTI KASASTOYIANNI
DRAWINGS: STELIOS DASKALAKIS
PRINTING-BINDING: PERGAMOS S.A.